MICHAEL LANDON

THE CAREER AND ARTISTRY OF A TELEVISION GENIUS

BY DAVID R. GREENLAND

Michael Landon: The Career and Artistry of a Television Genius

© 2014 by David R. Greenland

All rights reserved.

No portion of this publication may be reproduced, stored, and/or copied electronically (except for academic use as a source), nor transmitted in any form or by any means without the prior written permission of the publisher and/or author.

Published in the United States of America by:

BearManor Media

4700 Millenia Blvd.
Suite 175 PMB 90497
Orlando, FL 32839

bearmanormedia.com

Design and layout by Valerie Thompson

ISBN—978-1-62933-549-0

TABLE OF CONTENTS

A TRIBUTE . . . 1

ACKNOWLEDGMENTS . . . 3

FOREWORD . . . 5

PREFACE . . . 7

INTRODUCTION . . . 9

CHAPTER 1:   THE DREAMER . . . 11

CHAPTER 2:   GO WEST, YOUNG MAN . . . 17

CHAPTER 3:   THE PONDEROSA . . . 27

CHAPTER 4:   THE LITTLE HOUSE—PART 1 . . . 47

             THE LONELIEST RUNNER . . . 65

PHOTO GALLERY . . . 91

CHAPTER 5:   FATHER MURPHY . . . 103

CHAPTER 6:   THE LITTLE HOUSE—PART 2 . . . 109

             LOVE IS FOREVER . . . 113

             SAM'S SON . . . 117

CHAPTER 7:   THE HIGHWAY . . . 121

CHAPTER 8:   THE END . . . 145

             WHERE PIGEONS GO TO DIE . . . 146

             US . . . 148

BIBLIOGRAPHY . . . 153

EPISODE INDEX . . . 157

GENERAL INDEX . . . 161

ABOUT THE AUTHOR . . . 169

DEDICATED TO:

TO THE LANDON FAMILY
Past, Present and Future

A Tribute

At a time when the most cherished staples of TV entertainment are crime and car crashes, here's a courageous fellow daring to go against the grain by portraying an angel who performs acts of charity. What a wild notion! Are we really ready for anything that radical, that revolutionary? Are we prepared to give up our beloved karate kicks to the groin, exploding helicopters and the mating sounds of two pickup trucks colliding?

Of course I devoutly hope that we are, and that there's still a place on the tube for Michael's kind of programming, with its emphasis on real human values. In a world where all things frightful are beamed straight into our homes the instant they happen, we need Michael's weekly injection of goodness and decency as desperately as the diabetic needs his insulin.

ORSON WELLES
1984

Acknowledgments

David Dortort with the author, 1994
Photo by Barry Craig

This book would not have been possible without the assistance and/or encouragement of Doug Cameron, Barbara Douglass, Sandy Grabman, Karen Gray, Cleo Greenland, Paul Greenland, Steve Homan, Jeff Kadet, Andrew J. Klyde, Dennis Korn, Cindy Landon, Boyd Magers, Susan McCray, Michelle Morgan, Ben Ohmart, Janet Pease, Paula Rock, James Rosin, Valerie Thompson and Lanny Tucker.

Thanks to Mary Ann Bauman of the Michael Landon Fan Club, and to Harry Flynn, Michael Landon's longtime publicist, who authorized the club's newsletter. Thanks also to Vicki Christian, editor of *Bonanza Gold* magazine, who was kind enough to interview me regarding my history of the series.

Special thanks to the late David Dortort, creator and executive producer of *Bonanza*, who graciously invited me to his home for an extensive interview and contributed the foreword to my book about his television classic. In the letters and telephone conversations we exchanged up until his death in 2010, Mr. Dortort shared several insightful and positive recollections of working with Michael Landon.

There was one biography of Michael Landon published during his lifetime, a slim volume of questionable value that he said he had no intention of reading. Since his passing there have been no less than nine books either about the man, or in which he figures prominently. The most significant of these are *Michael Landon: Life, Love & Laughter* by Harry Flynn, Pamela Flynn, and Cindy Landon (1991) and *Conversations with Michael Landon* by Tom Ito (1992), both essential reading for any admirer of the man. Of further interest are *I Promised My Dad* by Cheryl Landon Wilson and Jane Scovell (1992), *Prairie Tales* by Melissa Gilbert (2009), *The Way I See It: A Look Back at My Life on Little House* by Melissa Anderson (2010), and *Confessions Of A Prairie Bitch: How I Survived Nellie Oleson and Learned to Love Being Hated* by Alison Arngrim (2010). Many thanks to all of these writers for sharing their memories of working and living with a truly unique individual.

Note: The photographs appearing in this book were originally distributed for publicity purposes and were obtained from various collectors and memorabilia dealers. The author claims no ownership rights to these illustrations.

DAVID R. GREENLAND
AUGUST 2014

Foreword
by Cindy Landon

My husband, the extraordinary Michael Landon, has been gone for more than twenty years. As sad and unfortunate as that is, it makes me happy to know he has never been forgotten. His work as an actor, writer, producer and director continues to entertain, inspire and touch people all around the world. Episodes of *Highway to Heaven, Little House on the Prairie* and *Bonanza* are always playing somewhere, on television or home video. Michael would be honored to know that his messages of love, understanding and hope have endured.

I am grateful that one of Michael's greatest admirers has devoted an entire book to a serious study of his productions, and I hope readers will appreciate David Greenland's efforts as much as I do.

I had the privilege of observing Michael create magic on countless occasions, whether he was at home writing or on set working on both sides of the camera. It was a pleasure to relive those times in the pages of David's book, as well as a bittersweet experience to be reminded of the many beloved co-workers who have passed away in recent years—Merlin Olsen, Moses Gunn, Kevin Hagen, Richard Bull, Ted Voigtlander and "Buzzy" Boggs, to name only a few.

In Michael's words, "I believe that we can all make our own miracles."

Keep laughing and loving! Find your passion and follow your dreams! To my husband, Mike, that's what life is all about.

Cindy Landon
August 2014

PREFACE

I was fortunate to experience much of television's golden age firsthand, when the majority of programming consisted of Westerns. At one point there were more than three dozen on the air, but I faithfully watched only three: *Gunsmoke, The Rifleman*, and, most of all, *Bonanza*, in part because, like the Cartwright boys, I was one of three brothers. All of us enjoyed the antics and heroics of Dan Blocker's Hoss, as most viewers did, but what we young buckaroos wanted most was to see Michael Landon's Little Joe spring into action.

There is a famous saying: Don't meet your heroes—you'll only be disappointed. I prefer to believe that did not apply to Michael Landon. To quote from a memoir I wrote the day after his untimely passing in 1991, "Michael Landon was the only celebrity I ever wanted to meet. Although I have been a fan since the tender age of nine, or thereabouts, this desire occurred not in the youthful days of exaggerated hero worship, but several years later, when I noticed that a *Bonanza* episode written and/or directed by him was something special."

While I do not remember the first time I saw Michael Landon, I know the exact date he first moved me: January 28, 1962. In "The Storm," episode #85 of *Bonanza*, Joe Cartwright plans to marry a young woman who, in keeping with one of the show's traditions, dies before the final credits roll. Rather than walk stoically into the sunset like any other TV cowboy would have done, Joe does not hide his grief. As an actor, Landon was not afraid to reveal his character's vulnerability, and the effect was both admirable and striking. "We are not afraid to show our feelings," producer David Dortort said later that season. "We have made more people cry than anybody in the business." And more often than not, it was Landon who made the audience feel, particularly after he began to write and direct.

My wife and I never missed an episode of *Little House on the Prairie, Highway to Heaven*, or anything else in which Landon was involved, and it was no secret among friends, relatives, and even a few casual acquaintances, that I considered him the most creative person in the television industry. One morning in 1979, driving to an appointment in Beverly Hills, the friend I was riding with pointed out a handsome estate and said, "Remember all those Bill Cosby records we used to listen to? That was his place once." He paused for effect before adding, "That's where your hero Michael Landon lives now. Want to stop and say hello?" "Yeah, right," I replied. "Besides, he's probably out shooting in Simi Valley."

In 1990, when the telefilm *Where Pigeons Go to Die* was in production, I received a business-related call from a woman in Kansas who, though unaware of my high regard for Landon, said, "Guess who I saw today? Michael Landon! He's here making a movie." "I don't suppose you talked to him," I ventured. "No, he was too busy," she replied. "And he seemed to be tired." I remembered that final remark a few months later, when my wife informed me that a friend had actually met Michael and Cindy Landon while skiing in Utah shortly after Christmas, but that "he didn't look well." Everyone knows the rest of the story.

I wrote letters of appreciation to Michael Landon on a couple of occasions—after the broadcast of his *Bonanza* landmark "Forever" in 1972, and the poignant *Little House* episode "Remember Me" in 1975—never expecting a reply. The man, I knew, was simply too busy. At least the letters were never returned, so I like to think he may have read them eventually.

After poring through a substantial archive of printed material, viewing nearly all of his appearances prior to *Bonanza*, and studying virtually everything he wrote and wrote/directed, I feel almost as if I had met Michael Landon. He certainly made his mark, leaving behind an unforgettable visual bounty for all of us that will doubtlessly never be equaled.

DAVID R. GREENLAND
AUGUST 2014

INTRODUCTION

This is not a book about the private life of Michael Landon. If there is an exception, it is only when he used incidents from it to enhance his art. Even the most high profile figure, whether they are a president or an entertainer, deserves the right to keep their personal space off-limits to the general public. Everyone should be known only by their public actions and whatever thoughts they choose to share with the rest of the world. Landon was no exception, yet he became perhaps the most scrutinized television personality in the history of the medium. Ironically, a man so opposed to judging others was unfairly judged all too frequently, often by people who never met him. To the end of his life, he castigated tabloid journalism—rightly so. It may be only natural for one to develop a certain measure of curiosity about what a favorite performer does behind the scenes, but if a fan sincerely respects that performer, there is a line that should not be crossed. Avoiding the gossip rags is an excellent place to start. (Considering Landon's staggering amount of activity—acting, writing, directing, producing, recording two solo singles and two albums (with his *Bonanza* co-stars), hosting community service specials, narrating nature documentaries, making personal appearances on telethons and at rodeos, participating on game shows and variety programs, sitting for countless filmed and print interviews, raising children—my one curiosity has always been: When did he sleep? No wonder he said he was fond of rising with, or even before, the sun.)

Like any creative person of genuine substance, Landon, more often than not, communicated chiefly through his work, be it his convictions regarding education or ecology, politics or religion. He believed in nurturing the family institution and strengthening its place in society, but above all he stressed the importance of love, a theme that runs continuously throughout the 330 hours of programming he produced. Of course, there are many other Landon hallmarks, written and visual, scattered consistently among the more than 300 hours of television he wrote and/or directed. That such a monumental achievement has never before been examined in detail is a situation this book seeks to remedy.

In addition, until now very little has been written about Landon's accomplishments as an actor before *Bonanza*, or outside his three classic series, but nearly all of them are discussed here. It becomes apparent while viewing any appearance he made prior to landing the role Ben Cartwright's youngest son that he had, in the words of David Dortort, "the most highly intuitive set of natural acting responses I've seen in a young actor." Consequently, Landon's portrayal of Little Joe emerged fully formed, whereas it took his three co-stars a while to develop their characters. Blessed with a wide range of acting skills—the most vital of them believability—he was able to avoid being typecast, transitioning comfortably and credibly into the boots of farmer Charles Ingalls and the modern garb of Jonathan Smith.

Genius is a word subject to many interpretations, as well as a term used far too loosely in the world of entertainment. One definition is "a great mental capacity and inventive ability, especially great and original creative ability in some art, science, etc." With an IQ of 159, Michael Landon was an authentic genius, and he used that gift to make discoveries where no one else thought of looking. As the late Ted Voigtlander, a director of photography, once said, "Many writers can 'see' things that maybe you can't photograph. Well, after getting to know the camera and the lenses, Mike can write things that you can actually do."

Michael Landon was concerned with making this world a better place, and shared his vision with us for over three decades. Recognizing—and celebrating—the filmed legacy he left behind is the purpose of this book.

DAVID R. GREENLAND

Chapter 1
The Dreamer
(1936–1955)

Landon, circa 1956

> "I spent my whole childhood dreaming.
> It was my escape."
> — Michael Landon to Tom Ito, 1990

Michael Landon not only refused to allow the dismal realities of his early life to prevent him from becoming one of the most successful and beloved icons in popular culture, he bravely tapped into those sour memories while creating a body of work still unmatched in the world of television. In his youthful daydreams he envisioned himself as such disparate figures as a pediatrician, superhero, soldier, cowboy, movie star and champion athlete. What no one—including Landon—could have foreseen was the former Eugene Maurice Orowitz of Collingswood, New Jersey, as an undeniable rarity in the entertainment industry: lead actor, writer, director *and* producer.

The future Michael Landon was born on Halloween, 1936, in Forest Hills, New York, the second child of Eli Orowitz, in charge of east coast publicity for Hollywood's RKO Radio Pictures, and Kathleen "Peggy" O'Neill, who three years earlier had given birth to a daughter, Evelyn. Both of Landon's parents possessed a variety of talents—Eli the author of a book about commercial broadcasting, Kathleen a former dancer and comedienne—and were enamored of Broadway. Unfortunately, how they differed became more important than what they had in common. Eli was a gentle, thoughtful man of the Jewish faith, whereas his younger wife was a loud, rather unstable Irish Catholic. "My mother committed suicide every other week, never accomplishing it," Landon told Dr. David Viscott during a televised interview in 1990. "I think I was eleven before I realized you put food in the oven and not your mother's head." Able to see the humor in his mother's staged attempts to kill herself, he incorporated these incidents into a couple of his future scripts.

By the time the Orowitz family moved to Collingswood in 1941, Peggy was embittered by having to trade a career in show business for motherhood, and Eli had lost his job with RKO and was managing a chain of New Jersey movie theaters. "I had parents who were children," Landon said, "and they needed someone to help them, to make decisions for them. When I was nine-years-old I went in and got my dad's job back that he had quit, that I knew he needed to have back but was too proud to do it."

While Peggy encouraged Evelyn to consider becoming an actress, she had little use for Michael, whom she seldom missed an opportunity to belittle and once chased out of the house with a kitchen knife. Little wonder he felt closer to his father. "I forget what it was I'd done," Landon said, "but it wasn't anything important. But my mother was extremely angry and wanted him to do something. I could hear her screaming in the other room at him, screaming at him to do something. Well, he was so frustrated he came into the room and didn't know what to do, and hit me. He wore a little pinky ring and it cut my lip. And he cried. And he left the room, and I thought that was great because I saw that he loved me."

To escape the chaos at 632 South Newton Lake Drive, Landon would retreat to a cave he had carved out in Newton Lake Park, conveniently located across the street from his house. Supplied with snacks, canned goods and comic books, he would spend hours daydreaming, imagining himself as anyone but Eugene Orowitz and anywhere but Collingswood, New Jersey. On occasion he would actually leave home. "I used to go to Philadelphia and stand in line with the bums, with dirty clothes on and a smear on my cheek, and a face that hadn't been washed in a week—as Edgar Guest would say—and stand there and get tons of money from people going into Gimbels Department Store. And then I'd take all of the rest of the guys because it's easier for a kid to get money than it is for an older person. And then we'd all go and buy a bunch of Philly cheese sandwiches and sit around and then go back and do it again. And I'd do it all weekend and sleep in a flophouse. And I was twelve." The memory of this activity would inspire Landon's creation of the Albert Ingalls character on *Little House on the Prairie* in 1978.

Much of Landon's semi-autobiographical 1984 film *Sam's Son* was based on his relationship with Eli and, to a greater extent, how he developed into an outstanding thrower of the javelin in high school. Thanks to an almost obsessive regimen of practice—including knocking the slats out of the family's picket fence—and despite his thin frame, he built up a powerful left arm and, in 1954, set a distance record of more than 183 feet. This accomplishment resulted in a scholarship offer from USC in Santa Barbara, which was fortuitous considering that Landon graduated 299th in a class of 301. Although blessed with a genius level intellect, he felt the best way for a small, unpopular Jewish kid to fit in with a predominantly Gentile student body was to become the class clown. "I studied hard, but I couldn't get good grades," Landon revealed several years later in a public service announcement promoting a video seminar entitled *Where*

There's a Will, There's an A. A strong advocate for education, he agreed to allow the program to continue being broadcast after his death.

Landon's days as a master of the javelin were short-lived. Convinced that his impressive strength was related psychologically to the then uncommon length of his hair—a result of seeing a hirsute Victor Mature as the Biblical strongman in the 1949 film *Samson and Delilah*—he suddenly lost his "magic" when a gang of goons from the football team held him down and cut it off. Not one to give up easily, Landon was determined to duplicate his personal best, practicing so vigorously that he tore a ligament in his left arm, putting an end to his days as a college athlete and student.

By this time, Landon's sister Evelyn—now calling herself Vickie—had moved to Los Angeles and was enrolled in classes being conducted by noted acting instructor Estelle Harmon. Landon, then working in a department store warehouse, teased his sister and a fellow student about how foolish their aspirations struck him. In response, the fledgling thespians dared him to audition and see if he could do any better. He accepted their challenge and so impressed Harmon with his naturalistic approach to the craft that he was invited to join the class. Landon, whose only experience had been playing a Japanese houseboy in a Collingswood production of *The Bat* when he was in junior high, was appreciative but not sure acting was in his future.

A fellow warehouse employee who was hoping to break into show business asked Landon if he would help him try out for the talent school run by Warner Bros. Studio, performing a scene from *Home of the Brave*, a play by Arthur Laurents concerning bigotry in the military. For the 1949 film adaptation, the persecuted soldier was portrayed by black actor James Edwards, but in the original stage version he was Jewish. Landon's co-worker did not want to take on the intense role in the two-man scene, so it fell to Landon to do the more serious emoting. His effective characterization resulted in his being admitted to the school. The co-worker returned to the warehouse.

Feeling that perhaps acting was not such a bad idea, Landon took a job pumping gas at a service station across the street from Warner Bros., hoping to interact with some of the studio executives who could be helpful in furthering his career. He eventually signed with

Bob Raison, an agent who advised him to change his name to something more theatrical and memorable than Eugene Orowitz. Landon's first suggestion was Michael Lane, which Raison vetoed. The Screen Actors Guild already had someone by that name registered, a character player who, coincidentally, was, like Landon, about to appear in a number of television Westerns. Raison proposed Michael London, which his client regarded as too stuffy, instead settling on Landon after a perusal of the phone book.

Although he seemed to be on his way, Landon would never totally embrace the often superficial Hollywood lifestyle, due largely to an incident involving his father which occurred, ironically, outside the gates of Paramount Studio, where he would soon attain stardom on *Bonanza*. Eli, preparing to join his offspring in California, had set up a job interview with some of his old associates, who had moved from RKO to Paramount, located on the adjoining lot. Landon drove his father to the appointment and waited while Eli went to check in with the guard at the studio gate. Nearly half an hour later, Eli returned to the car, visibly shaken. His "friends" said they were too busy to see him. Landon decided then and there that he "wasn't going to expect anything from anybody that had to do with business, and I wasn't going to worry about somebody's friendship if it affected what I did for a living. Unlike my father, I wasn't going to take garbage from anybody."

Landon's first professional job was not in film or television but in a stage production of *Tea and Sympathy* at the Players Ring Theater in Hollywood. His performance drew critical raves, and casting directors around town, especially in television, took notice, leading to parts on *Passing Parade* and *Crossroads*, a dramatic anthology on ABC. He was also cast in his first Western, making a brief appearance as a cavalry soldier in "Decision," an episode of the Warner Bros. series *Cheyenne* that would air in early 1956.

Michael Landon's life on the Hollywood prairie had begun.

Chapter 2
Go West, Young Man
(1956–1959)

Landon as Joe Cartwright

> "I have a lot of moxie, and I had it from the moment I came to this town. And you have to have that if you're going to make it in this business. You have to be willing to hang around outside the door of the agency and do the scene from the time that agent hits the front door or until he or she gets to their car."
>
> Michael Landon, 1990

During 1956, Michael Landon appeared on no less than half a dozen different television series and was seen very briefly in the James Cagney and Barbara Stanwyck feature *These Wilder Years*, released that August. By the end of the year he had a wife and an adopted son to support, which necessitated his finding other work between acting jobs. Before he could rely solely on the entertainment industry for his livelihood he was a process server and blanket salesman, and had labored in a car wash, ribbon factory and cannery—a variety of positions not unlike those that would be held by his Jonathan Smith character on *Highway to Heaven*.

Landon's episodes of *Cheyenne* and *Crossroads* aired a few days apart in January, followed by a second segment of *Crossroads* and roles on *Telephone Time, Wire Service,* and two appearances on the ABC series *The Adventures of Jim Bowie*, one of ten Westerns then being offered by the three major networks. In the first, "Deputy Sheriff" (09-28-56), Landon is cast as Jerome Juventin, a barefoot, dark-skinned Cajun who speaks broken English and is skilled at swordplay, as Little Joe Cartwright would be in early episodes of *Bonanza*. Coincidentally, the sheriff is portrayed by none other than *Bonanza*'s Ray Teal, Virginia City's sheriff, Roy Coffee. The second, "The Swordsman" (12-14-56), finds Landon as a hot-headed Frenchman (Armand De Nivernais) who wears a top hat and challenges Bowie (Scott Forbes) to a swordfight that turns into a fistfight Armand loses. In these episodes, Landon, still shy of twenty-years-old, is both brooding and intense, a template for many of the characters he would soon play in numerous Westerns, with a focus one expects to see in more seasoned professionals.

Landon's star was definitely in ascendency throughout 1957, beginning with roles on *The 20th Century-Fox Hour, Cavalcade of America, State Trooper, DuPont Theater,* a third installment of *Crossroads, General Electric Theater,* and a second visit to *Telephone Time* ("Fight for the Title") in which he was cast as Kid Lombard, a skinny but tenacious would-be prize fighter. Rather than a cocky scrapper, Lombard is a sympathetic figure, with a high-pitched voice and subdued manner that is a marked contrast to most of Landon's previous characterizations. He is entirely convincing in what could easily have been a one-note performance. Among the other actors are future *Bonanza* guest stars George Brenlin and Don Haggerty, whose careers their young co-star would soon eclipse.

On March 29, the CBS dramatic anthology *Schlitz Playhouse of Stars* broadcast "The Restless Gun," a Western starring veteran film actor John Payne as Britt Poncett (renamed Vint Bonner for *The Restless Gun* series), a wandering cowboy who needs to warn an old friend that an escaped prisoner is out for revenge. Standing in Britt's way is a punk gunman named Sandy, whom Landon brings to amusing life with a mixture of insolence and charm. Sandy smokes, plays cards, talks tough and shoots a window out, but Britt remains unaffected, succeeding in dunking the antagonistic youth backwards into water not once, but twice. Landon could not have known it at the time, but this appearance was one of the most important moments of his life, key to his achieving enduring stardom.

A more infamous appearance, one that would never quite fade from the public's memory, was his first significant film, American-International's *I Was a Teenage Werewolf*, released in June. Low budget horror films combining teenagers and monsters were a staple of drive-in theaters in the 1950s, and it was perhaps inevitable that a young actor as handsome and obviously talented as Landon would eventually add at least one to his resume. Technically, he was beyond high school age but looked sufficiently youthful to be believable as the troubled ("I burn easy...People bug me"), ill-fated Tony, beating out Jack Nicholson for the role. To counter his explosive temper, Tony visits a psychiatrist who hypnotizes him to a regressive, primitive state—and presto! A teenage werewolf! With a supporting cast of such solid character actors as Whit Bissell, Malcom Atterbury and Guy Williams (all destined to guest on *Bonanza*), as well as the fact that Landon's performance is superior to his younger co-stars and the material, *Werewolf* is a notch above most examples of the genre. Realizing he would forever be linked to the film, Landon would joke about it in interviews, particularly the scene in which Tony's father advises him not to eat pork chops raw. Thirty years later, he would spoof *Werewolf* on an episode of *Highway to Heaven*.

As the year progressed, Landon worked steadily: *Alcoa Theater*, two episodes of *Suspicion, The Court of Last Resort*, another installment of *Schlitz Playhouse of Stars*, and *Matinee Theatre*. But the Old West continued to call: *Dick Powell's Zane Grey Theater* ("Gift from a Gunman," as a light-haired admirer of an aging gunslinger attempting to retire), but especially *Tales of Wells Fargo*, on which he made three appearances. In "Shotgun Messenger" (05-07-57), he was cast as Tad Cameron, a polite and enthusiastic Wells Fargo recruit victimized by a pair of outlaws responsible for crippling his father. (One of the villains is Kevin Hagen, who would become best known as *Little House*'s Doctor Hiram Baker.) The next month, June 10, Landon was back on the show in "Sam Bass," playing a mustachioed train robber named Jackson and second-billed behind guest star Chuck Connors. For the second time, *Bonanza*'s Ray Teal (as a Texas Ranger) and the soon-to-be Joe Cartwright cross paths. The producers were sufficiently impressed by the job Landon did in "Shotgun Messenger" that they brought back the Tad Cameron character in "The Kid" (11-18-57), giving him top billing and briefly putting him in a jail cell. It would not be the last time viewers would see him misunderstood and behind bars. At the end of the 1957-58 season, *Wells Fargo* was the number three program in the country, giving Landon his greatest exposure on the home screen to date.

Early 1958 found Landon in what was fast becoming where audiences were most likely to see him: the television Western. By year's end he would guest on ten episodes of seven different series, including *Schlitz Playhouse of Stars* ("Way of the West"), *Cheyenne, Wanted Dead or Alive, Tombstone Territory,* and two episodes each of *Trackdown, The Texan* and *The Rifleman*. He also had parts on *Studio One* and two installments of *Alcoa Theatre*, the second a pilot for a series called "Johnny Risk," co-starring Lew Ayres (a future guest star on *Little House: A New Beginning* and *Highway to Heaven*) and which Landon was later relieved never went into production. Another unsold pilot in which he co-starred was *Luke and the Tenderfoot*, whose cast included Edgar Buchanan, Lee Van Cleef, Charles Bronson and Leonard Nimoy.

"White Warrior," the March 11 episode of *Cheyenne*, was Landon's first appearance in an hour-long Western. It was also his largest role to date, allowing him to exhibit a wider range of emotions. As a white Apache slave named Alan Horn he faces the bigoted passengers of a wagon train being led by Cheyenne Bodie (Clint Walker), yet helps save them from an Indian attack. More often than not, Landon preferred to perform his own stunts, and here he gets the chance to show off his athletic skills in a knife fight.

The first of Landon's two episodes of *Trackdown*, "The Pueblo Kid" (04-04-58), opens with him (as Jed Daws, who at one point wears his jacket with the collar upturned, as Joe Cartwright would do) checking his gun and polishing off a glass of whiskey. Although known as the title character, a notorious gunslinger, it later develops that he has never killed anyone, telling Texas Ranger Hoby Gilman (series star Robert Culp) he only wanted that reputation because he has always been a nobody. He avoids shooting his nemesis (George Brenlin from "Fight for the Title") and takes his gun off for good by the final curtain.

Landon does not give up the gun in "The Martin Poster," the September 6 premiere episode of Steve McQueen's *Wanted Dead or Alive*. As Carl Martin, one of two murderous brothers (the other, Andy, played by Nick Adams, later of *The Rebel*), he has his first role as a truly bad character. Josh Randall (McQueen), of course, triumphs over the brothers, wounding Carl and killing Andy. Townsman Tom Wade is portrayed by the late, great Dabbs Greer, who was to gain lasting fame as Reverend Robert Alden on *Little House on the Prairie*.

On September 17, Landon had one of his more interesting roles in "Rose of the Rio Bravo" on *Tombstone Territory*. As Barton Clark, Jr., the son of a wealthy man, he enters the jail of Marshal Clay Hollister (Pat Conway) dressed like a dude and announces that he wants to be a deputy. Hollister tells him he has no need of one, but that he can work as a handyman and jailer. When Clark accidentally shoots a gun at the ceiling, Hollister is definitely convinced the young man is not lawman material. Clark is good natured and obedient at first, but falls under the spell of Rose (Kathy Nolan of *The Real McCoys*), a conniving woman outlaw Hollister arrests. After helping Rose to escape, Clay flees with her to Los Angeles, where he is ultimately shot. When he says he wants to write his will and leave everything to Rose, a newspaper editor informs him he is not dying. A memorable episode, made more so by Landon's engaging performance.

The same is true of "End of a Young Gun," the October 14 installment of *The Rifleman* that, because of Landon's role, series star Chuck Connors regarded as "special." In fact, Landon is given prominent billing, in capital letters, in the final credits. As Will

Fulton, member of an outlaw gang on the run, Landon stops to rescue Mark McCain (Johnny Crawford) from falling off a cliff. Will is successful, but breaks his leg in the process. While recuperating at the McCain ranch, he has an opportunity to watch the peaceful domesticity of Lucas (Connors) and son Mark, and even meet an attractive girl named Ann. When Mark says he thinks it would be fun to be an outlaw, Will disabuses him of that notion. Naturally, the rest of the gang shows up at the ranch, but Will joins Lucas in gunning them down. Affected by living a normal life, Will decides to turn himself in to the law, vowing to return to Ann.

In "The Hemp Tree," the November 17 episode of *The Texan*, Nick Ahern (Landon), in love with the daughter of a disapproving sheriff, is falsely accused of bank robbery and flees to Mexico. He is pursued by Bill Longley (series star Rory Calhoun), who convinces him to return and clear his name. Fortunately, the guilty party is right-handed, and Nick is left-handed, as was Landon. Not a particularly noteworthy episode, but Landon gets to woo co-star Susan Anderson and slug it out with Calhoun.

Less than two weeks later, Landon made his second *Trackdown* appearance on November 28 ("Day of Vengeance") as Jack Summers, a young ex-con not far removed from the character he played on *The Restless Gun*. In other words, a swaggering, cigarette-smoking malcontent determined to cause trouble. This time, however, Landon is able to develop a more fully realized role, thanks to a story that is not entirely predictable.

In addition to all of this activity on the Hollywood prairie in 1958—including several episodes not aired until early the following year—Landon was cast in three theatrical features, including *Maracaibo*, his first job on a foreign location (Venezuela) as well as the first time he was filmed in color. In the Paramount production, starring and directed by Cornel Wilde, he is billed fifth (as Lago Orlando) in a cast of nine. Despite being based on a novel by the gifted Stirling Silliphant, the chief asset of this largely forgotten film about a raging oil fire was the scenery.

Nor was Landon given much to work with in *High School Confidential,* a low budget cautionary tale of teenage delinquency and marijuana dealers released by in June by MGM. Billed tenth out of eighteen, he does not appear until twenty minutes in, playing

Steve Bentley, president of a car club known as the Rangers. His seven scenes total less than five minutes of screen time, and he is not listed at all with the rest of the cast in the closing credits.

Better was *God's Little Acre*, based on the best-selling novel by Erskine Caldwell and directed by Anthony Mann. Landon more than holds his own among an imposing roster of pros: Robert Ryan, Buddy Hackett, Jack Lord, Tina Louise, Fay Spain, Aldo Ray and Vic Morrow, the latter five all future guests on *Bonanza*. With a high, tremulous voice, large thatch of white hair, and eyes made darker by contact lenses, he stands out as Dave Dawson, an albino who allegedly has the ability to locate buried gold by using a divining stick. He proposes marriage to co-star Fay Spain, but is eventually chased away at the point of a shotgun for giving the destitute Georgia farmers false hope. (As an inside joke during the 1985 *Highway to Heaven* episode "Going Home, Going Home" Landon searches for water with a divining stick, stumbling and shuffling like his Dave Dawson character did more than 25 years before.)

Landon worked on at least eight different television programs in 1959, one of which would provide him with full-time employment as an actor for the next fourteen years. Before that, he appeared in episodes of *Playhouse 90, Johnny Staccato,* and the modern Western *U.S. Marshal*, but it was the Old West that was destined to be the setting of his professional life, beginning with a pair of shows that had been filmed the previous year.

For his second and final *Zane Grey Western Theatre*, Landon co-starred opposite Michael Rennie in "Living is a Lonesome Thing," broadcast on New Year's Day. As yet another young cowpoke with a hair-trigger temper (Vance Coburn), he quits the family ranch, changes his name, joins another outfit, and is ultimately killed by his own father.

Two days later, on the syndicated *Frontier Doctor* ("Shadows of Belle Starr"), directed by Western veteran William Witney, series star Rex Allen dissuades Landon (Jim) from joining an outlaw gang, but not until after he has participated in a robbery and been bitten by a rabid dog.

Landon returned to Steve McQueen's *Wanted Dead or Alive* for "The Legend" (03-07-59), filmed mainly at Vasquez Rocks, a familiar Western location, and co-starring Victor Jory. (Landon and Jory would be reunited at the Vasquez site for the first two-part *Bonanza* episode, "Ride the Wind," seven years later.) During a search in the desert for Spanish gold, temperamental Clay McGarrett (Landon) complains to Josh Randall (McQueen) that he has never been able to please his father (Jory) in 22 years, but succeeds when helping to defeat the outlaws who are firing on them.

Vasquez Rocks also figures prominently in "The Man from Brewster" (04-24-59), Landon's second role on *Tombstone Territory*. As Chris Anderson, he is second-billed to John Carradine's crooked Sheriff Bins, who is attempting to frame Chris for the robbery of a gold shipment, or so it seems. Landon gets to appear disheveled, dirty and hatless, and participate in a surprise ending that is effective due mainly to his convincing performance.

In his return visit to *The Rifleman* ("The Mind Reader"), again co-starring with John Carradine, he is given little do but sit in a jail cell for what is one of his smallest guest shots. However, by the time the episode aired (06-30-59), Landon had already signed on for steady work in a series of his own. In early 1959 there were more than 25 Westerns on the three major networks, nearly all of them a half hour in length, yet NBC felt there was room for another—a one hour series called *Bonanza*.

That July, while Landon was shooting the premiere season of *Bonanza*, his second and final starring role in a theatrical feature was released by Columbia Pictures. Based on a hit song by the Kingston Trio released the previous fall, *The Legend of Tom Dooley* was very much a product of its time, intended to not only cash in on the record's popularity but also take advantage of the public's apparently insatiable thirst for Westerns. The film was helmed by Ted Post, director of more than fifty episodes of *Gunsmoke*, then the number one show on television. Not surprisingly, *Dooley* plays like an expanded television episode, shot at such familiar locations as Thousand Oaks, Iverson Ranch, Columbia Ranch and even the phony exterior Dodge City set at Paramount being used by *Gunsmoke*. The cast, too, is made up of several actors working primarily on television (Jo Morrow, Richard Rust, Jack Hogan, Dee Pollack, Ken Lynch, Ralph Moody, Cheerio Meredith), many of whom would later appear on *Bonanza*. Landon is top billed as the title character, and is first seen sitting pensively on horseback as the camera slowly zooms in before the opening credits roll. As the doomed Confederate soldier, he is able to display a greater range of his acting skills than on television, adopting a passable Southern accent as part of his process. In the closing scene, Dooley rides into the shadows with a pair of lawmen. And Landon was already headed toward lasting fame.

Chapter 3
The Ponderosa
(1959–1973)

Landon on location with the *Bonanza* crew, 1963

"Lorne and Dan, God bless 'em, were absolutely the two most terrific guys to do a series with over fourteen years.
I love those years. They were great."
Michael Landon, 1979

Television's second longest running and arguably most popular Western may never have existed if not for the unyielding convictions of its creator and executive producer, David Dortort. A novelist and screenwriter, Dortort was the first writer in Hollywood to become a producer, specifically of the John Payne series *The Restless Gun*, which lasted for two seasons on NBC. The network was anxious to begin airing shows that it also owned, and in early 1959 told Dortort that if he had any ideas, he could create anything he wanted. He thought of adapting the legend of King Arthur and the Knights of the Roundtable to the Old West's Sierra Nevada mountains, an intriguing notion that NBC executives felt had possibilities. However, they balked at the cost when Dortort said envisioned the show as being in color. Nor did the producer's notion of casting unknown actors as the leads have much support. Dortort refused to be swayed, insisting that it would be foolish to film the majestic scenery in color, and that television was capable of making its own stars, as it had done with the *Gunsmoke* cast and innumerable others. Believing firmly in his concept, he proposed sharing in the financial risk if the network would do the series his way. NBC ultimately agreed, perhaps due in part to its warehouses of unsold color television sets.

For Ben Cartwright, the owner of the Ponderosa Ranch and patriarch of the frontier family, Dortort chose Lorne Greene, whom he had observed guest starring on *Wagon Train*, which, like *The Restless Gun*, was produced at Universal Studio. Pernell Roberts, whose performance in the Randolph Scott film *Ride Lonesome* had impressed Dortort, was cast as Adam, the eldest son, and Dan Blocker, who had guest starred on *The Restless Gun* several times, was Hoss, a role created specifically for him. For the part of the youngest Cartwright, Little Joe, Dortort saw Michael Landon in the pilot for *The Restless Gun* and had not forgotten him. "For some reason no one had ever signed him for a regular series," the producer said. "I fixed that." (Dortort once remarked that he had made the mistake of killing off Landon's *Restless Gun* character. When reminded years later that he had not produced the pilot, and that Landon's character did not die, Dortort, with a smile, replied, "I've done so much television I can't remember who died and who didn't!") After Landon passed away, Dortort said, "I liked him for a number of reasons. First, he was an absolutely, amazingly handsome young man. And he had an air. You had to automatically like him."

For Michael Landon, the thrill of finally securing steady employment as an actor was bittersweet. Only two days before being offered *Bonanza*, his father suffered a fatal heart attack while eating soup in a Los Angeles restaurant. At the time, Eli Orowitz, abandoned by his former colleagues in the entertainment industry, was working in a shabby second-run movie theater. Father and son had grown closer in recent years, and Landon was devastated. "I still use him in acting," he said. "All I have to do is think of him and I can cry. Or, if I want to portray fury, no problem. I just think of how people were dishonest with my dad." Over the years, Lorne Greene was to become something of a surrogate father for Landon, and Dan Blocker the brother he never had.

NBC wanted *Bonanza* on their 1959 fall schedule, and the series was rushed into production that March. The pilot, "A Rose for Lotta," was written by Dortort and filmed mainly on the Paramount lot, which had one of the few two-story Western town sets that could pass for Virginia City, Nevada. Central to the plot is a plan to kidnap Little Joe, who gets a couple of chances to demonstrate his fencing skills, as well as his fondness for the ladies, in this case guest star Yvonne De Carlo. In one scene, when her character asks Joe why they refer to him as little, he says that he is in comparison to Hoss. David Dortort, a student of history, admitted he knew of the existence of an 1898 ballad entitled "Little Joe the Wrangler," but that it was not his inspiration for the name of the youngest Cartwright.

A couple of months after *Bonanza*'s debut on September 12, Dortort reluctantly confessed that he felt Landon and Blocker were likely going to emerge as the most popular members of the cast, a prediction that was to prove correct. First season episodes that either feature them together or separately stand up particularly well today. As the Ponderosa's resident hothead and heartthrob, Little Joe is involved in a majority of the action and romance, and Landon is very effective handling both in "The Julia Bulette Story." After observing Landon's tearful emoting in the episode's death scene, played with guest star Jane Greer, an admiring Dortort told a reporter visiting the set, "Mike didn't play that scene; he lived it."

Conversely, Landon and Blocker successfully portray Cartwright brothers and their outlaw doubles in "The Gunmen," the first of the series' many comic Hoss and Joe misadventures. It is also a treat to watch them interact in "The Last Hunt," a relatively more sober installment filmed extensively at California's Big Bear Lake. The first episode with supernatural overtones, "Dark Star," has Joe falling for a peculiar gypsy woman, with a somewhat hammy performance by Susan Harrison that only serves to make Landon's thespian abilities seem all the more impressive.

Bonanza was initially scheduled on Saturday evening opposite CBS's hugely successful *Perry Mason*, and despite the fact that Westerns continued to attract a large audience (nine of the top twenty shows), it did not begin to catch on with viewers until the 1959-60 season was nearly over. Feeling the ratings were reasonably improved, NBC renewed the series for a second year, but in the same Saturday time slot. By the end of the season, *Bonanza* had risen to number seventeen, while *Perry Mason* fell from number ten the previous year to number sixteen. The popularity of the Cartwrights was obviously growing, not only because the show had the novelty of being in color, but mainly because of, as Dortort explained, "the excellence of the cast." All of the actors portrayed a distinctly different character: Ben, the father figure; Adam, the intellectual; Hoss, the amiable strongman; Little Joe, the mischievous yet quick tempered romantic. As the latter, Landon soon developed into the most multi-dimensional Cartwright, more than sufficiently talented to teach sign language to a young woman who is both deaf and mute ("Silent Thunder"), bungle a humorous bank robbery with Hoss ("Bank Run"), contend with a gang of ruthless bandits ("The Gift"), and endure being accused of murdering a pregnant girl ("The Secret").

In the fall, NBC moved *Bonanza* to Sunday, where it rapidly surged upward to become the second highest rated program of the 1961-62 season, trailing *Wagon Train*, but only by a slim margin. Landon is memorable in such varied episodes as "The Lonely House," "The Friendship," "Day of the Dragon," "The Tin Badge," "The Storm," and "The Mountain Girl," but on a personal level his greatest achievement was "The Gamble," his first writing credit.

In January 1962, with no new script to shoot, production of *Bonanza* was on the verge of shutting down. Landon, not wanting to find himself unemployed, spent a weekend dashing off a story about the

Carwrights being jailed for robbery and murder. "It was written in longhand and only thirty pages," Dortort said, "but I felt it had possibilities." With writer Frank Cleaver, Landon worked on the script even as the episode was being filmed, beginning on January 19, a Friday, and not wrapping until the following Friday. The story includes touches of humor (Hoss's appetite and weight), sentimentality (Ben, Hoss and Adam exchange memories of Joe and reflect on things taken for granted as they wait to be hanged), and plenty of action (Joe smashing through a window, an army of Cartwright hands riding to the rescue). Appropriately, "The Gamble," which aired on April 2, was directed by William Witney, known for his expertise with action sequences.

When asked about his creative habits several years later, Landon said, "I'll think about the characters for weeks. I may lie on the bed and stare at the ceiling for hours. Then, when it's all straight in my head, I work very fast, getting it down on paper in two days." Eager to branch out beyond writing, he began paying more attention to how directors set up different shots, and which camera lenses were used for certain scenes and effects. "Mike was a real workaholic," said Dortort. "He almost never left the studio. He wanted to be part of every part of the filmmaking process."

Starring on a hit television show, flying off on the weekends to make personal appearances, anxious to expand his artistic horizons—all while raising a family—began to take its toll on Landon. "I was an insecure guy," he said thirty years after *Bonanza*'s debut. "All of a sudden I was a big star, and that's tough to handle because you don't know why. So, therefore, when you're insecure and you don't know why, you tend to strike out and act like you think a star should act. And if you have any brains, you outgrow it." Fortunately, he could turn to Lorne Greene, one of the few industry people he respected, for counsel. He also immersed himself in making *Bonanza* better by doing a lot of his own stunts and trying to add color to the work of other writers. "The producers were often so busy they would send us scripts with scenes marked *interior saloon*," he said. "There would be no dialogue. So I started writing dialogue for these two-minute scenes. I tried to inject some humor into them, like having Dan Blocker do something silly, like throw me out a window at the end of a scene. It was fun, and it added something special to the show." What irritated him once he began writing entire scripts on his own was the industry's assumption that they were ghostwritten. "After my first script, I heard that several writers around town called another writer who's done a lot of *Bonanza*s. 'Who wrote that script for Landon?' they asked him. "Oh, he wrote it himself, did he? Well, then who polished it, who put it into shape?' They were dumbfounded to learn that Mike Landon, the kid in the cowboy suit, had done it all himself. Every last word."

During the next few seasons, Landon did no credited writing for *Bonanza*, but delivers numerous outstanding performances in such episodes as "The First Born," "The Quest," "The Last Haircut," (reportedly Dortort's favorite Joe story),"Five into the Wind," "Twilight Town," "Calamity Over the Comstock," "The Quality of Mercy," "Alias Joe Cartwright," (playing his double) "Bullet for a Bride," "Invention of a Gunfighter," "Between Heaven and Earth," (inspired by his and Dortort's aversion to heights), and "The Trap," to name only a dozen. Little wonder he was honored with the Silver Spur Award for being the Most Popular Western Star by the Western Writers of America in 1964.

By the seventh season (1965-66), *Bonanza*'s second as the number one show on the air, Pernell Roberts was gone and more screen time was available for the remaining three Cartwrights, even as stories increasingly involved the problems of the guest stars. The amount of location shooting at Lake Tahoe's Incline Village also increased. Landon shines in such episodes as "Five Sundowns to Sunup," "The Code," and "Peace Officer," but most noteworthy is the series' first two-part installment, "Ride the Wind," with Joe joining the Pony Express. Behind the scenes, Landon was beginning to collect valuable writing tips from John Hawkins, who would later contribute to *Little House on the Prairie* as both a writer and associate producer.

Landon returned to writing the following season, collaborating with Rik Vollaerts on "Ballad of the Ponderosa," which aired on November 13, 1966. With actor/singer Randy Boone strolling around Virginia City as he sings a tale of how Ben Cartwright is responsible for the hanging of Boone's father, the episode is slightly melodramatic but not entirely predictable. Scenes involving Hoss's appetite and Ponderosa cook Hop Sing (Victor Sen Yung) becoming irate over a character's lack of appetite were no doubt contributed by

Landon, who was to often reference Hoss's girth, and include Hop Sing, in many of his future scripts. Directing the episode was William F. Claxton, destined to work extensively with Landon on *Little House on the Prairie* and *Father Murphy*.

Claxton also directed "Joe Cartwright, Detective" (03-05-67), a comic episode written by Landon, but based on a story by Oliver Crawford. Peppered with a musical soundtrack straight out of *Dragnet* and *Batman*, this escapade of Hoss and Joe's attempts to nab a pair of bank robbers is played strictly for laughs. Known for his frequently wacky sense of humor, the chance to turn out a genuinely amusing script was doubtlessly a challenge Landon gladly accepted.

Joy Dexter came up with the story idea for "The Wormwood Cup" (04-23-67), and Landon assisted her in writing the teleplay. One of the best moments of the eighth season, a woman offers a reward to anyone who will kill Joe in a fair fight although a jury has determined that he killed her brother in self-defense. In addition to a couple of surprise twists, the episode is significant for director Claxton's use of shadows and camera angles, devices that would become potent tools in Landon's hands after he began directing.

In its ninth season, *Bonanza* added David Canary as ranch foreman Candy Canaday to the cast and, in general, began to emphasize action over drama. Not coincidentally, Robert Blees, a line producer on the recently canceled war series *Combat!*, was hired to temporarily replace production manager Kent McCray, busy helping David Dortort launch *The High Chaparral*. Even if stories were more plot than character driven, Landon figures prominently in such episodes as "The Conquistadors," "Night of Reckoning," "Blood Tie," and "Pride of a Man." Yet his participation on the show this year was more important behind the camera, as both a writer and, for the first time, a director.

William Jerome submitted a story ("Six Black Horses") in which a friend of Ben's steals money from corrupt New York politicians and plans to invest it in Nevada. Landon helped Jerome with the rather pedestrian seriocomic script, enlivened chiefly by guest star Burgess Meredith. His first totally self-written contribution to the show, "It's a Lot of Bull," was rejected by NBC on the grounds that the Indians in the story knew how to speak English, which did nothing to improve Landon's opinion of those on the business end of the industry. "How many years has Hollywood been making pictures where cowboys and Indians speak to each other in English?" he asked. "We certainly should be able to take this much dramatic license. You begin to get the feeling that somebody's just trying to think of something to write down, so they can send a memorandum."

With the April 14 episode, "A Dream to Dream," Landon was finally able to see a story and script that were entirely his own produced for *Bonanza*. Directed once again by William F. Claxton, it is one of the few segments from the 1967-68 season to emphasize character development rather plot. On a trip to purchase horses for the Ponderosa, Hoss becomes involved with a bitter, alcoholic rancher (Steven Inhat) who mourns his dead son to the point of ignoring his wife (Julie Harris) and other two children (Johnnie Whitaker, Michele Tobin). Hoss, of course, is moved by the family's plight and does what he can to bring them together. Two of what were to become Landon's favorite subjects—children and love—combine at the conclusion, when Whitaker tells Hoss, "We love you." (Landon would recycle this script eleven years later for the 1979 *Little House* episode "Someone Please Love Me.")

While at Incline Village to shoot the November 19 episode "Showdown at Tahoe" the previous summer, Landon was finally able to wrangle a directing assignment from David Dortort. During a press conference, a reporter asked the producer if any of the actors were going to direct, and when Dortort responded in the affirmative, Landon pressured him to specify when that would occur. The producer waffled a bit before publicly promising his actor a seat in the director's chair that season.

The result was "To Die in Darkness" (05-05-68), also written by Landon, in which Ben and Candy are held captive in a deserted mine shaft by ex-convict John Postley (James Whitmore), wrongly sent to prison because of Ben's testimony. This avoids being a potentially stagnant episode, both dramatically and visually, thanks to expertly paced storytelling, convincing performances, and imaginative direction. Landon favors close-ups at significant moments, unusual camera angles, interesting establishing shots, and a striking use of shadows and light. An overhead shot of Ben and Candy lying helplessly at the bottom of the shaft segues neatly to Postley thrashing restlessly in bed. In the closing sequence, filmed in Los Angeles' Bronson

Canyon, Ben places and understanding hand on Postley's back as the camera pulls back to a crane shot, lending the episode an eloquent coda. In 1990, Landon recalled, "I remember when I first started directing on *Bonanza* I had to con my way into getting the job because no one would believe for a minute that Little Joe had the ability to direct a show. And even the crew wanted to help me right from the very beginning because I did want to do things differently." David Dortort immediately recognized Landon's penchant for exploring new avenues of expression as a director. "Quite often," said the producer, "someone who has not been strictly tutored in the way things are typically done can discover new concepts and new solutions, particularly if they are observant, and original in their thinking. Michael was both. I know he said *Bonanza* was better than any film school he could have attended, and he certainly proved that."

In the first episode filmed for the series' tenth year, "The Passing of a King" (shown fifth, 10-13-68), Landon and guest star Jeremy Slate engaged in a knockdown, drag out fight that Slate recalled as one of the roughest he had ever done. "Yeah, we did that ourselves," he said. "Mike always liked to do his own stunts, and he was pretty damn good, too!" As impressive as the staged fisticuffs were, Landon's major contribution that season was his sole credit as writer and director, an episode of which he was proudest.

In "The Wish" (03-09-69), Hoss helps a black family tend to their farm and deal with bigots in a nearby town, unintentionally offending the patriarch, Sam (Ossie Davis), by being overly solicitous. At the time, there was widespread racial unrest in the wake of Martin Luther King's assassination the previous year. "Mainly," Landon explained, "I wanted to get across the idea to whites just why black people are angry and frustrated, and I wanted to cool some of the backlash. One black writer saw the show and he said to me, 'You've gotten so close to what it's like to be black, I could hardly believe it was written by a white man.' For me that was my Emmy." In what was to become one of the regular traits of a Landon production, Sam seems to materialize out of the darkness to confront the two men who have beaten his youngest son. After Hoss and the boy bid each other an emotional farewell, the camera slowly moves in on a candle burning in an open window, stopping as the wind blows out the flame. "I did a lot of wishing when I was a kid," Landon revealed, "and I always lit a candle before I made my wish." The episode won a Bronze Wrangler Award from the National Cowboy Hall of Fame and Western Heritage Center in 1970.

With two momentous episodes he both wrote and directed to his credit, attentive *Bonanza* viewers could rightly expect a Landon creation to be special or, at the very least, unique. The latter is true of the "Dead Wrong" (12-07-69), the first of three offerings in the eleventh season, with Landon's customary mention of Hoss's appetite and a token scene for Hop Sing. An all-out comedy, Hoss and Candy find themselves mistaken for bank robbers in the town of Sunville, and end up having to stage Hoss' death, with the help of the town loudmouth. The guest stars include such amusing stalwarts as Arthur Hunnicutt, Mike Mazurki, Robert Sorrells and John Carradine. As an inside gag, Landon gave brief, non-speaking roles to some his in-laws.

Rather than start "It's A Small World" (01-04-70) with an ordinary shot of Ben and Deputy Clem Foster (Bing Russell) playing cards in the Virginia City jail, Landon opens with close-ups of the two, accompanied by ominous music and dialogue, then reveals the men to be playing for nothing but matchsticks. Suddenly, a dwarf named George (Michael Dunn in an unforgettable performance) with a painted face bursts in and announces desperately that his wife is having a baby and needs help. A sad but ultimately uplifting episode focusing on one of Landon's favorite targets: prejudice. When George says he wants to move on because he is tired of being ridiculed for his small stature, Ben tells him that if he stays and waits until everyone realizes all people are the same, it will make things easier for the next person who looks different. (Landon revamped his script for "Little Lou," a 1982 episode of *Little House: A New Beginning*.)

"Decision at Los Robles" (03-22-70) is pure action and suspense. In the title town, Ben kills a self-appointed sheriff who has shot him in the back, after which Joe and some of the braver residents hide Ben from the sheriff's vengeful son and ranch hands. Although a fairly straightforward tale, Landon manages to elevate it with interesting camerawork. Instead of showing Ben and Joe simply riding into Los Robles, Landon starts with a shot of a woman sweeping debris off an upstairs porch and onto a man's head. Later, when the sheriff's son smashes a mirror, the camera cuts to the bartender polishing the saloon mirror.

Landon neither wrote nor directed "A Matter of Circumstance," the April 19 episode that ended the 1969-70 season, but in what is nearly a one-man performance, he should have at least been honored with an Emmy nomination. When Joe's arm is seriously injured by a frightened horse, he struggles to survive, going so far as to contemplate amputating the shattered limb himself.

Landon may have been denied an Emmy, but composer David Rose, whose poignant scores would become Landon's "secret weapon" for notably enhancing *Little House on the Prairie* and *Highway to Heaven*, earned one for "The Love Child" (11-08-70). Written and directed by Landon, by now considered in some circles to be *Bonanza*'s not-so-secret weapon, the episode can easily be seen as representative of the melancholy and even tragic themes that would inform much of his future work. Unlike most of what passes for creativity in today's popular culture, Landon never emphasized style at the expense of substance. "The Love Child" has equal measures of both. In lesser hands, the story of a dying unwed mother and her small boy being rejected by her father could be mawkish melodrama, but the acting by guest stars Carol Lawson, Will Geer and Josephine Hutchinson—as well as Lorne Greene—is brilliantly understated and believable, doubtlessly due in large part to Landon's perceptive direction. Michael-James Wixted, as the young son, observes the adults' trauma with puzzlement rather the expected tears, also a credit to Landon's vision. The first scene begins with a blood smear on a glass slide, then light from a window falls and remains on restless hands as the mother and her doctor speak. Close-ups of hands would continue to be a Landon trademark throughout the rest of his career behind the camera. In addition to the now almost obligatory jab at Hoss's appetite, again involving Hop Sing, there are two other Landon traits employed, specifically the use of rain and expressions of love. A memorable *Bonanza*, with nary a fist or gunfight. (This script was also the basis for the *Highway to Heaven* episode "Child of God" in 1985.)

For "Terror at 2:00" (03-07-71), Landon returned to the action and suspense route. Bigoted assassins posing as newspaper men come to Virginia City intent on disrupting the signing of a treaty with the Paiutes. After stealing a Gatling gun, they set it up in an upstairs hotel room and wait for their targets to arrive. A close shot of flowers—a visual device of which Landon became very fond—and the pleasant sound of a harmonica begin this otherwise tense episode on a disarming note. As with any successful script of this nature, there are moments of humor, supplied mainly by Hoss and Deputy Clem's attempts to get their pictures taken. In the end, Joe succeeds in rescuing a captive Hoss and blasting the head villain with a shotgun, but not before the Gatling gun chews up the hotel room. The camera pulls up to show the destruction, gun smoke still hanging in the air. Earlier, Landon superimposes a flashback sequence over a close-up of an eye mesmerized by a clock's swinging pendulum.

"Terror at 2:00" would not have stood a chance of being aired in 1968, which is when the Landon-penned "Kingdom of Fear" was originally scheduled to be shown. Because of Martin Luther King's assassination that April, it (and several other shows on all three networks judged to be too violent) was shelved until April 4, 1971. Filmed at Incline Village during the summer of 1967, and directed by action specialist Joseph Pevney, the Cartwrights and Candy are forced to work on a chain gang from which escape is impossible. Of course, the resourceful stars come up with a way for Joe to break out and go for help. This being a Landon script, an element of sadness is added when one of the freed prisoners bids adieu to his dead wife at her gravesite. (David Canary's presence in the cast is billed as a "special appearance." Inspired by Landon's efforts behind the camera, he had left the series after the eleventh season in an unsuccessful attempt to produce a series of his own.)

A few weeks before, Landon directed "The Stillness Within," written by Suzanne Clauser and one of the series' most beloved episodes. After being blinded by an explosion, a bitter Joe wallows in self-pity and initially rejects Miss Dobbs (the incomparable Jo Van Fleet), the woman attempting to teach him how to live without sight. When he is able to see again he discovers that she is also blind. Devastated, he bursts out in tears and sinks to his knees, one of many powerful scenes in another *Bonanza* ignored by the Television Academy of Arts and Sciences. In addition to successfully meeting the challenge of portraying a sightless person, Landon stages nearly every scene as a work of art. Joe lunging for the bottle of nitroglycerine that blinds him is shot in slow motion; the camera pulls back from a close-up of a doctor's mirrored headset; the arrival of Miss Dobbs begins with a close shot of her hand on the Ponderosa's door knocker; the scene of Joe learning to pour coffee ends with the camera pulling back to show the living room dark but the dining area illuminated by a dim shaft of light; Joe's hand blocks the camera lens before cutting to a scene of him learning to walk down the stairs; the camera lingers on the contents of a jar of preserves that has fallen on its side; the sun shines through a window as Joe's face moves into the darkness, then emerges into a close-up of his eyes; when Joe sees himself in a mirror, he places his hands on the reflection to make certain it is real.

Landon wrote and directed three episodes for *Bonanza*'s last full season (a fourth story, "Bandits, Thieves and Kidnappers," was never produced), as well as the last with Dan Blocker, but he was evidently involved controversially in the production of others. A few years later, David Dortort said, "It got bad because Landon developed very quickly as a good director. Then, as an actor, he began to criticize what he thought were errors being made by other *Bonanza* directors. They'd come to me and say, 'We spend most of our time arguing.' It was the same with Mike Landon, the writer. He'd challenge nearly every line, every scene, every setup in other writers' scripts. Everything would halt for endless story conferences on the set, and I finally had to use Dan Blocker as an intermediary to say, 'Let's get on with the damned thing.' It got increasingly bitter toward the end."

Much later on, Dortort clarified his remarks: "Mike only wanted the show to be as good as it could be, and he was extraordinarily gifted. The problem was not his ego, but his obsession with improving everything. 'Good enough' was never acceptable to him, and that's an admirable quality, no question. But in television you don't have the luxury of time. There's never enough time to get everything done as close to absolutely perfect as possible. Making a show, or a motion picture, is usually a democratic process, and that frustrated Mike. We had our disagreements, but, I must tell you again, they had nothing to do with ego, our personal feelings for one another." In 1986, when asked about his need for total control of his productions, Landon said, "I just don't feel that you can make a really terrific product if there's a large committee second guessing each other all the time. I like input from the people I'm working with, but I don't want a whole bunch of people who really aren't a part of the company in the first place."

The degree to which Landon had "developed very quickly as a good director" (as well as a writer) was evident in "Don't Cry, My Son," which aired on his 35th birthday (10-31-71). With the exception of Ben's humorous quip about the birth of Hoss having been "a labor pain," this is a particularly dark, sad story. When a doctor's wife loses their baby in childbirth, she leaves her husband, who was helping with another woman's delivery at the time. The doctor snaps and kidnaps his patient's baby in hopes that it will convince his wife to come back to him, leading to a tragic, realistic conclusion. Landon begins the episode benignly, with a close-up of a squirrel gnawing on nuts in front of the Ponderosa, which is quite a contrast to the last shot: the camera pulls back and up to show the doctor and his wife on the ground, surrounded by darkness. During the simultaneous delivery scenes, Landon cuts back and forth between the two women, one woman's hands gripping her husband's, the other the bedposts. In similar set-ups clearly becoming one of Landon's favored signatures, the hands of the doctor's wife are the focal point of the shot as she packs to leave, and a chess game between Ben and Deputy Clem starts on a close-up of the latter's hand. Landon's trenchant use of light to lend atmosphere to certain moments is evident when Ben attempts to reason with the doctor's wife, the murky hotel room matching the mood. This episode introduces some provocative new music composed by David Rose that would later be used for one of Landon's highest achievements before *Bonanza* ended.

In "He Was Only Seven" (03-05-72), writer/director Landon again deals realistically in tragedy, though he opens with another jab at Hoss's weight. A young boy is shot and killed during a bank robbery, and Joe and adopted Cartwright son Jamie (Mitch Vogel) join the boy's grandfather in tracking down the outlaws. The grandfather, masterfully portrayed by Roscoe Lee Browne, happens to be confined to a wheelchair, making the task more arduous. Rather than come across as one-dimensional stereotypes, the members of the outlaw gang are given sharply defined characteristics in a relatively short length of time, one of Landon's considerable gifts as a writer. The leader's lack of redeeming qualities, for example, is demonstrated by showing what a negative influence he has over his own boy. As always, there is no shortage of skillfully conceived direction, the robbery in particular, with quick-cut edits of Joe being slugged, a bank teller being shot, and the boy shot at but not shown being hit. We are made aware of the outcome only when Joe returns from shooting at the outlaws and sees Jamie cradling the boy's body. The doctor tends to the boy in silhouette, behind a backlit sheet, and when the boy dies, there is a close-up of the coins he has in his limp hand. Later, the expected sound of a gunshot is replaced by the crack of a wagon wheel going over a rock, there is a transition shot from fluttering leaves to a flickering campfire, and the episode ends with the camera once again pulling back to an overhead shot. Finally, it is worth noting that a saloon girl is called Alice, a name that, for an unknown reason, Landon would use frequently in his writing.

"The Younger Brothers' Younger Brother" (03-12-72), the last misadventure with Dan Blocker written and directed by Landon, is genuinely hilarious. A trio of bumbling misfits, led by the always entertaining Strother Martin, is released from prison after twelve years, intent on resuming their criminal ways. Hoss, unfortunately, is identified as one of their brothers. Landon liberally peppers the proceedings with comic banter and numerous sight gags, including the use of dynamite to blast out of—and into—jail, tearing up the floor of shack to find guns that are actually under a mattress, and gunfire knocking down a fence instead of the bottles and cans being shot at.

After *Bonanza*'s thirteenth year ended in April 1972, NBC announced that the show, which had slipped from ninth place the previous season to twentieth, would be moving from Sunday to Tuesday. In preparation for the change, the network began airing reruns as *Ponderosa* in the new weeknight slot. Although he was opposed to NBC's decision, David Dortort was cautiously optimistic that viewership might increase, as *Gunsmoke*'s had when it switched from Saturday to Monday five years before.

Landon wrote "Forever," the two-hour premiere episode of *Bonanza*'s fourteenth season, in which Hoss was to have been married, but on May 13 Dan Blocker, shockingly, succumbed to complications following routine gall bladder surgery. He was only 43. "After Dan's death," said Lorne Greene, "I didn't see how the show could continue. I said to my wife, 'That's it—it's finished.' I know Michael Landon felt the same way." "For me," Landon said, "Dan's death was like losing a brother." Just as he had drawn on the memory of his father to convey sorrow as an actor, Landon did the same after Blocker's passing, saying, "Whenever I have to cry, I think of Dan." According to the late Mark Landon, Blocker said, "Your father is the best director I ever worked with."

Hoping to at least partially make up for Blocker's absence, Dortort rehired David Canary, and Tim Matheson signed on as an ex-con paroled in Ben's custody. Two episodes were filmed while Landon revised "Forever," which would still open the season on September 12, ironically the same date the series debuted in 1959. He completed the final draft of a 96-page script detailing 265 shots (including some later revised, others not used) on June 7. In retrospect, it was his first unquestionable masterpiece, one that could have served as a fitting swansong for *Bonanza*.

After thirteen seasons of almost countless courtships, Joe, the Ponderosa's resident Romantic, makes it to the altar with Alice Harper (Bonnie Bedelia), whose shiftless brother, John (Andy Robinson), is a gambling addict. Unfortunately, John is in debt to a quartet of thugs led by a malevolent "gentleman" named Damion (Larry Golden). When John suggests that his sister's wealthy in-laws might be willing to pay what he owes, the four miscreants accompany him to Joe and Alice's home, where the new (and pregnant) Mrs. Cartwright is alone. She refuses to turn over her jewelry, and is attacked by Damion's mute enforcer, Hanley (Roy Jenson). Damion shoots John dead. The gang leaves with the jewels, stored in a music box once belonging to Joe's mother, and set fire to the house. Joe, Candy and Jamie arrive too late to save anyone who might still be alive. After his badly burned hands are sufficiently healed, Joe rides off to grieve by himself. He encounters a saloon girl who has his mother's music box, then returns to the Ponderosa to enlist Candy's help in tracking down the killers. Appropriately, Damion is the only one to die instead of being captured, drowned by his own sadistic henchman, Hanley.

"Forever" is a veritable cavalcade of Michael Landon's substantial gifts as an artist: close-up shots of hands and at dramatic moments;

unexpected camera movements; panoramic sweeps; overhead shots; imaginative use of mirrors; interesting establishing and transitional shots; creative soft to sharp focus scenes; smooth tracking shots within a scene rather than traditional cutting; and especially the way light itself becomes a character, used for contrast and enhancement. The lively barn dance Joe and Alice attend, as well as their light-hearted parting at the hotel door, is followed immediately by the dark scene in which John slips from the shadows and poignantly admits to Alice that he has made a mess of his life and she is right to send him away. Many such scenes, in fact, are played with a minimum of—or no—dialog. We learn of Alice's fate only by a simple comment made by Deputy Clem.

The episode is also a compendium of several of the most memorable moments ever presented by *Bonanza*: Joe's first mention of Hoss no longer being among the living; Alice and Joe strolling happily through the woods, ominously descending into darkness as though their future is being forecast; Joe's profile superimposed on the landscape as the camera tracks to the high country; Joe in a full beard to indicate the passage of time; Joe and Candy's shootout with two of Damion's men, shown in two quick, dramatic cuts.

Two scenes in particular rank among the most emotionally powerful of the series, difficult for even the most devoted fan to watch. In the first, Joe and Ben tearfully embrace in the burned-out ruins of Joe's house, a sequence that reportedly had some crew members reaching for a handkerchief. No one had to wonder which departed cast member the actors were remembering. In the following scene, after Joe has departed on his search for solitude, a high angle long shot shows Ben alone in the room, his back to the viewer. He gently touches something on Joe's dresser before leaving. As David Rose's wistful rendition of his 1970 "Big Bonanza" theme swells, the camera moves in slowly to reveal framed portraits of Hoss and Joe.

Landon explained that what he wanted "Forever" to do "was try to make it a catharsis for everyone, not just the audience but for us, too—to try to incorporate a sense of loss. We mention Hoss's death very simply, in passing, the way it happens in real life; there's no discussion of how or when. I'm sure that some people would rather have a whole hour memorial to Dan, but we just couldn't do that. We tired to do what we thought he would have wanted us to do."

Years later, when asked how he regarded the episode, all David Dortort said was, "Beautiful."

Although "Forever" drew strong ratings in the show's new time slot, TV Guide claimed that "droves of viewers resented" the death of Alice Cartwright, even though NBC had announced a few months before that Landon had planned for the character "to meet death later in the season," regardless of which Cartwright she married. (Coincidentally, Dan Blocker and Bonnie Bedelia had appeared together in the tenth season's "The Unwanted" three years before.)

On October 31, six weeks after "Forever" aired—and Landon's 36th birthday—that night's episode ("The Twenty-Sixth Grave," the first to be filmed for the season) came in at a dismal #53 in the ratings, trailing behind producer Norman Lear's *Maude* (a spinoff of the #1 *All in the Family*) and *Hawaii Five-O* on CBS and *Tuesday Movie of the Week* on ABC. Three days later, NBC canceled *Bonanza* and gave Dortort only a few days to close down his Ponderosa. Too stunned to announce the end of the show, he left it to Landon to handle the media. Although he had recently signed a production deal with network that gave him complete control over future projects, Landon shared Lorne Greene's resentment toward NBC's lack of respect for what had so long been one of the most successful series in television history. His sense of humor intact, he attended the press conference wearing a stunt harness that pulled him back into a pile of boxes, the "victim" of a shotgun blast.

Landon had written an additional five scripts for the final season, only two of which were filmed before the network axe fell, and broadcast after. (The unproduced teleplays were "A Poor Man's Treasure," "Barnaby" and "The Giant Killer.") In "The Sound of Sadness" (12-05-72), his affection for children and senior citizens is touchingly obvious in a simple story of an elderly widower's attempts to adopt a pair of runaway orphan boys. (Landon again uses the name Alice, this time for the man's deceased wife.) The episode opens with a typical Landon trademark—a close shot of guest star Jack Albertson's hands—and closes with another, "I love you," the first words spoken by a boy who has said nothing else during the entire show. Landon enjoyed working with many of the same actors throughout his career, in this case Carol Lawson (from "The Love Child" and "It's a Small World") and Dan Ferrone

("Don't Cry, My Son"). (This story was rewritten for the 1980 *Little House* episode "The Silent Cry.")

Bonanza's final episode, "The Hunter," was also Landon's last for the series, filmed on location in Arizona's Coronado National Forest and the Old Tucson movie set. A grim tale reminiscent of the classic *The Most Dangerous Game*, Joe is pursued through the wilderness by a deranged escapee from a military prison. The only moment of levity occurs during a brief final look at the interior of the Ponderosa ranch house, when Jamie points out an error in Ben's accounting ledger. The episode is bookended by overhead shots of the prisoner (Tom Skerritt) in jail cells. Production was plagued by unpredictable desert storms, but Landon makes this inconvenience work for him by capturing effective shots of an ominous sky and a rain-soaked ghost town.

"The Hunter" aired on January 16, 1973, bringing the Cartwright saga to a close after 430 episodes, fourteen of them directed by Michael Landon, and twenty-one he had either co-written or turned out by himself. He had helped considerably in making *Bonanza* a rarity in the world of television: a series that improved with age. And he was far from finished.

Chapter 4
Little House: Part One & The Loneliest Runner
(1973–1982)

Karen Grassle, Landon, Melissa Sue Anderson, Lindsay or Sidney Greenbush, Melissa Gilbert, Jack of *Little House on the Prairie*, 1974

"I want people to laugh and cry, not just sit and stare at the TV. Maybe I'm old-fashioned, but I think viewers are hungry for shows in which people are saying something meaningful.
Michael Landon, 1974

Landon's first post-*Bonanza* project was writing "Love Came Laughing," the premiere installment of NBC's short-lived anthology series *Love Story*. Bonnie Bedelia, Joe's ill-fated bride Alice Harper on *Bonanza*, headlined as an unwed mother named Alice Hartman. After airing on October 3, 1973, the episode was never seen again, and *Love Story* itself was history by January. Except for Landon's continued inclination to use the name Alice, the story was notable for a humorous scene in which a woman (Eileen Brennan) feigns a suicide attempt by putting her head in an oven, as Landon's mother had done on several occasions.

The previous spring, Landon's eldest daughter, Cheryl, had been seriously injured in a terrible auto accident, leaving her in a coma with little chance of survival. Landon remained at her bedside in intensive care for several days. "I promised God that if he would let her live, I would do something useful with my life," he said, "something to make the world a little better because I'd been there. Cheryl lived, and I've tried to keep that promise ever since."

Landon kept his promise by spending the bulk of 1973 working on three quality projects: two biographical telefilms and the pilot for what would become one of the most revered family series ever produced. *The Jackie Robinson Story*, about the life of the acclaimed Brooklyn Dodgers' second baseman, aired on NBC in 1974. Regrettably, it has not been seen since and is unavailable on home video. Fortunately, the second biopic, which debuted on February 22 that year, remains a visible example of Landon's directorial legacy. With excellent camera work by *Bonanza*'s Ted Voigtlander, *It's Good to Be Alive* is the inspiring account of how Roy Campanella, catcher for the Brooklyn Dodgers, recovered from a near-fatal car accident to become a coach of his team.

Landon begins with a shot of the real Campanella's hand as he writes; a collage of the ball player in action accompanies the opening credits. After being informed that the Dodgers are moving to Los Angeles, Roy (Paul Winfield) drives home on a rainy night, his thoughts illustrated by quick cuts to him in action on the diamond. The car spins out on the wet pavement and lands upside down, and Roy, staring out a window, continues to reflect back on his glory days as rescuers work to extricate him from the wreckage. In the hospital, Roy mutters the 23rd Psalm while being anesthetized. Landon segues from a close-up of a light in the operating room to light coming through a church's stained glass window while the congregation also recites the 23rd Psalm. A flashback to young Roy being told he is a child of a mixed marriage features a close shot of his mother's black hand and his father's white hand side-by-side. Following the operation on Roy's fractured fifth and sixth vertebrae, the camera pulls back and up to show him paralyzed and in traction. When pestered by a housefly (its movement captured by making the camera pivot dizzily from Roy's point of view), the immobile man's irritation is magnified by Landon's use of an extreme close-up of the insect crawling on Roy's face. More scenes of Campanella's feats on the ball field are intercut with sequences of his rehabilitation, aided by Sam, a physical therapist memorably played by Lou Gossett. Later, when the car carrying Sam and Roy crashes, Landon shoots the moment so effectively that the viewer is almost as surprised as the men. At the conclusion of a scene where Roy is coaching the team, the camera is placed at ground level to show dirt kicked up when a player slides into a base. *It's Good to Be Alive* was well-received, critics calling Landon's film "a moving portrait" and "rewarding viewing."

After *Bonanza* ended, Landon was deluged with offers for a new series, most of which he dismissed as junk. Among the proposals were series involving doctors, detectives, and even a man from outer space. Only two ideas intrigued him, one of which concerned a traveling newspaper man reporting stories about the people he met—which would much later evolve into Landon's last pilot, *Us*, in 1990—and a series based on the popular books by Laura Ingalls Wilder. He was leaning toward tackling the latter when producer Andy Fenady (*The Rebel, Branded*) approached him with the notion of doing an adventure show based on the exploits of writer Jack London. Some test shots of Landon in early twentieth century dress were done, but he ultimately decided to pass. He did, however, promise Fenady that he would give the project a chance if his next pilot for NBC, based on *The Little House on the Prairie* (the third of Wilder's nine memoirs), did not result in the standard initial order for thirteen episodes.

Producer Ed Friendly had been shopping *Little House on the Prairie* around to all the networks without success until the name Michael Landon was attached. NBC gave Friendly the green light, and production of the two-hour pilot began in January 1974, with a script by Blanche Hanalis, who developed the Ingalls saga for television, and Landon in the director's chair. Exteriors were filmed in Sonora and Stockton, California, depicting the snowy woods of Wisconsin and the windswept plains of Kansas, the landscape itself becoming a character. It was Landon's most elaborate—not to mention grueling—shoot to date, complete with his usual contrasting of shadows and light, close-ups of hands, and scenes observed from overhead. Unlike his portrayal of Joe Cartwright, Landon's Charles Ingalls plays the fiddle and smokes a pipe, but one cannot help but be reminded of his *Bonanza* character when he is seen on horseback, rifle in hand, being chased by a pack of wolves.

Easily stealing the show is Victor French as Isaiah Edwards, a widowed farmer who helps build the Ingalls cabin and stable, braves a blizzard to deliver Christmas presents to the Ingalls family, and is the most emotional after the army informs Charles that he is homesteading on Indian land and must move on. French, the son of Hollywood stuntman Ted French, embarked on an acting career with a bit part on *Lassie* in 1954, followed by appearances (usually as a villain) on such series as *Two Faces West, The Dakotas, The Virginian, Mannix, Daniel Boone, Gunsmoke, Rawhide, Mission: Impossible, The Waltons, Kung Fu*, and was Agent 44 on the sitcom *Get Smart* for five seasons. Most significantly, he guest starred in five episodes of *Bonanza*, meeting Landon for the first time. His theatrical features included a small role in *The Magnificent Seven* (1960), Elvis Presley's *Charro!* (1969), and John Wayne's *Rio Lobo* (1970). Isaiah Edwards was the first substantial role of his career, playing the character from 1974 to 1977, and reprising it for the final season in 1981-82. "I was surprised Michael remembered me at all," French recalled in 1985. "And then he had to fight for me, too. NBC wanted a 'name' as Isaiah. Fortunately, Michael stuck to his guns and it turned my career around. And my life."

Network executives had low expectations, but when the end result was previewed, the test audience gave *Little House* the highest score of any pilot in NBC's history. When broadcast on Saturday, March 30, ratings were sufficiently promising to warrant going ahead with a series. While Friendly wanted the show to remain faithful to the source material, Landon felt Wilder's stories were sometimes dull and often too depressing. Landon's vision of the series prevailed, and viewers never saw Charles Ingalls with a beard, or his daughters walking to school without shoes. Filming commenced in May on two soundstages toward the back lot of Paramount Studios, Landon's old *Bonanza* stomping ground from 1959 to 1970. Location shooting was originally planned to be done in Woodland Hills, but was quickly moved to the less populated Big Sky Ranch in Simi Valley, also a former "home" to *Bonanza*. The town of Walnut Grove consisted of fully constructed sets, built to resemble actual buildings, rather than the typical false facades seen in so many period productions. "Our show is probably the most authentic, visually, of any ever made about the Old West," Landon said. He also insisted the food, such as bread and pancakes, look as it would have in the previous century.

Little House on the Prairie has been inaccurately described as a children's program, and unfairly maligned as saccharine. To the contrary, it was a family show with frequently sad and even dark overtones, as well as a vivid and unabashed examination of the human condition and life on the Minnesota frontier. There was a trend toward less violent programming in 1974, and on Wednesday, September 11, *Little House* joined such series as *Apple's Way, Born Free, Sons and Daughters* and *The Waltons* as part of that movement. Only the latter ranked higher in the year-end ratings, with *Little House* coming in at an impressive #13. Landon initially thought the show would run for four seasons—which, as a testament to his creative instincts, were arguably its most consistently satisfying—but it lasted nine. Of the 200 episodes (including the final season as *Little House: A New Beginning*), Landon wrote 36 and directed 72 while also functioning as both actor and executive producer.

Unlike some Hollywood directors, Landon respected child actors (though understandably annoyed when they were not prepared for a day's shooting) and was directly involved with casting director Susan McCray in choosing his screen family. Cast as eldest daughter Mary Ingalls was Melissa Sue Anderson, whom Landon admitted reminded him of his first girlfriend. Alison Arngrim, eventually awarded the role of nasty Nellie Oleson, auditioned for the parts of both Ingalls girls, but it was Melissa Gilbert who would mature in front of the television audience as Laura, known affectionately to

Pa Ingalls as Half-Pint. Hers was the only screen test Landon showed to NBC. The twin daughters of actor Billy Greenbush, Lindsay and Sidney, alternated in the role of youngest sister Carrie, and classically trained actress Karen Grassle was cast as mother Caroline. Coincidentally, shortly before production began, Grassle had filmed an episode of *Gunsmoke* directed by none other than Victor French.

As he had on *Bonanza*, Landon continued to enjoy working with certain actors with whom he was familiar. Consequently, several of his fellow thespians landed regular or semi-regular roles on *Little House*: Karl Swenson as mill owner Lars Hansen, Richard Bull as storeowner Nels Oleson, Katherine MacGregor as Harriet Oleson, Kevin Hagen as Dr. Hiram Baker, Dabbs Greer as Reverend Robert Alden, Charlotte Stewart as schoolteacher Eva Beadle Simms, Ted Gehring as banker Ebenezer Sprague, Donald "Red" Barry as farmer Larrabee, and James Jeter as blacksmith Hans Dorfler. There were also a few special guest appearances in the first season, including *Bonanza*'s Mitch Vogel as Johnny Johnson in two episodes, Dan Blocker's son Dirk in one, and Landon's daughter Leslie in another.

Without question, Landon's selection of prolific composer David Rose to score *Little House* was crucial to the overall tone and emotional impact of the series. The main theme was first heard more than three years before in a January 1971 episode of *Bonanza* ("Top Hand"), and Rose would occasionally use other familiar musical motifs, or variations of them, from *Bonanza*. Regarding his work on *Little House*, he said, "It has nothing to do with western music. It's dramatic contemporary music done in a legitimate scoring fashion, which is almost a disappearing art." Rose was nominated for an Emmy four times during the run of the series, winning twice, in 1979 and 1982. (Similarly, cinematographer Ted Voigtlander was also awarded a pair of Emmys, in 1978 and 1979.)

Now involved in virtually every aspect of a series, Landon still managed to write three, co-write one and direct five of the first season's 23 episodes. By this time, viewers who had been paying attention were well aware of his unique gifts as a director, and though he maintained that directing was his main passion, it was as a writer that Landon distinguished himself most on *Little House*, several stories inspired by his real life experiences as a family man.

After directing "A Harvest of Friends" (09-11-74, written by producer John Hawkins and William Putnam) he again went behind the camera for "Mr. Edwards' Homecoming" (10-02-74), Victor French's first appearance as a series regular. Although written by Western veteran Joel Murcott, the name Alice once more pops up in a Landon production, this time used in reference to Isaiah's dead wife. A humorous transition shot cuts from French wailing his signature tune, "Old Dan Tucker," to Laura saying "ahh!" while being examined by Doc Baker. Landon switched gears to write "The Award," handing the directorial reins to William F. Claxton, who was to helm more Landon productions than anyone. Along with Lorne Greene, Claxton was one of the few people in the entertainment industry that Landon genuinely admired and trusted. As a rule, Landon preferred directing the episodes he had written, but not only did he have sufficient faith in Claxton's abilities to entrust his friend with "The Award," he does not even appear in it. Instead, Charles and Isaiah deliver voice-over dialogue as a long shot shows them—most likely Landon and French's stand-ins—riding away in a wagon.

"The Award" (12-11-74), the twelfth episode of the first season, is an interesting story of ethics and obedience that could easily have been thoroughly predictable, but not coming from Landon's imagination. Hoping to win a Webster's Dictionary by acing an exam, Mary borrows a history book from her teacher to study for the contest. While reading by lamplight, she accidentally sets fire to the Ingalls barn, destroying the book in the process. Upset, Caroline forbids Mary to take the exam. Feeling she has been too harsh, Caroline consults Reverend Alden, who tells her that family discipline is based on promises kept, for punishment or reward. In short, Mary cannot be permitted to participate in the contest. To buy a new history book for Miss Beadle, Mary works at Oleson's store, then appears to be taking the exam against her mother's wishes, which Caroline observes. When the dictionary is won by another classmate it seems as if Mary defied her mother for nothing, but Miss Beadle informs Caroline that Mary was not taking the exam. Instead, she was writing an explanation as to why she could not. Mother and daughter tell each other they are sorry, Caroline admitting she was too strict.

The beginning of the series' first two-part installment, "The Lord is My Shepherd," aired the following week, postponed from the week of Thanksgiving because the network felt it was too depressing. Nonetheless, this first episode to be written and directed by Landon was also the first landmark of the series. Melissa Gilbert later named it her personal favorite. After opening symbolically on a shot of a bird alighting on an egg-filled nest, Caroline reveals—wordlessly, as Alice Cartwright does in *Bonanza*'s "Forever"—to Charles that she is pregnant. Charles—like Joe Cartwright in "Forever"—worries that the house is not large enough, and, again like Joe, builds a cradle. To illustrate the passage of time, Landon shows the nest which began the episode filled with hatchlings. Caroline gives birth to a boy, and a jealous Laura tells Mary that she had prayed for another sister. Tragically, the baby dies. In the dimly lighted doctor's office, Charles and Caroline recite the Lord's Prayer as the camera pulls back and up to an overhead view. Laura takes the death the hardest, convinced her jealousy was responsible. After hearing Reverend Alden tell the congregation "if you rid yourself of evil thoughts and deeds, all things are possible," she asks him if God would grant a miracle if she prayed hard enough. Alden replies that the closer she is too God, the more likely He is to listen. Appropriately, Laura is shown, small and meek, from Alden's point of view in the pulpit. Taking the reverend's words literally, she decides to climb the highest mountain she can find to ask God to resurrect her dead brother. In a stunning shot, Laura is dwarfed by the landscape as she crosses a meadow toward the distant mountain. Charles and Isaiah take off on horseback to search for her. After praying for God to take her and return the baby to life, Laura awakens to the sight of a man, the sun shining halo-like behind his head. The man, named simply Jonathan, tells her it is his mountain, and that God must be behind in his chores for not answering her prayer yet. While waiting for a response from above, Laura rescues an injured dove, and Jonathan whittles a wooden cross with her name carved on it. He tells her that water is Heaven's tears, which can make things come alive again. The cross falls into a stream and is carried away. Laura tells Jonathan about her deal with God, saying He took her brother by mistake, that she was the one who had mean thoughts. A distraught Charles, emotional and bearded as Joe became during his search in "Forever," finds the cross Jonathan made, then spots the signal fire Jonathan suggests Laura light to attract God's attention. When she spots her father and Isaiah approaching, she tries to hide, but Jonathan tells her God sent the men because that is the way it has to be. He claims God told him. Laura tells Charles about Jonathan (Ernest Borgnine), who is nowhere to be seen, nor is the injured dove. Isaiah, an atheist, looks around, puzzled. The episode concludes with a close-up of the dove perched on a fir branch before flying away, a touching moment of television regardless of one's religious convictions.

Landon wrote the teleplay for "Plague" (01-29-75), based on a story he wrote with William Keys, and directed by William F. Claxton. Walnut Grove and the surrounding farms are threatened by cornmeal that has been fouled by rats infected with typhus, hardly a scenario that critics of the series could label saccharine. What saves the episode from being a mere disease-of-the-week show are a number of heartfelt scenes that were almost certainly devised by Landon: A farmer holds his dead son under a tree and tells Charles it is too nice a day for the boy to be in school; Charles tells Caroline that the plague keeping them apart reminds him of when they were courting under her parents' watchful eyes; a young girl (Leslie Landon) tells Charles she knows she is going to Heaven because she is dying in church; Charles reminds Isaiah that he is family.

"To See the World" (03-05-75), written by Gerry Day and directed by Landon, is a somewhat atypical episode in that it involves Isaiah and Johnny Johnson (Mitch Vogel's second and final appearance on the show) rather than the Ingalls. The town of Mankato is actually the *Bonanza*'s Virginia City set at Paramount, and David Rose's theme for Johnny is the same one used for Vogel's Jamie Cartwright. Similarly, the piano music heard in the saloon was heard in "Forever." All in all, director Landon must have felt as if it was old home week.

The second season of *Little House* dropped a few notches in the ratings, but that was no commentary on the quality of the series, which, if anything, was better than its freshman year. With the characters and their situations firmly established, the writers—including Landon—were free to explore new ideas. During the course of the season, Mary learns that she needs glasses, Ted Gehring is introduced as banker Ebenezer Sprague, and most importantly, Isaiah Edwards is married.

Landon directed all four of his scripts, as well as two others, beginning with the season opener, "The Richest Man in Walnut Grove" (09-10-75). When the company that has bought the lumber mill goes bankrupt, Charles discovers he will not be getting the back pay he was counting on. Caroline can tell by observing his body language from a distance that something is wrong. The family listens to Charles play his fiddle in the dark house, dimly illuminated by only the fireplace, and Laura tells Mary she can always tell how their father is feeling by the way he plays. The Ingalls clan pulls together and benefits from the kindness of neighbors, with the exception of storeowner Harriet Oleson and the two bratty Oleson children, Nellie and Willie. Charles insists that the family do business with the Olesons on a cash only basis, telling Laura any job that helps someone make their way in the world is a decent job. The episode is filled with several memorable scenes: Laura punching Nellie in the nose, Charles' admiration of Caroline when she helps with the plowing, the family paying their bill at the store dressed in their Sunday best, and the long-suffering Nels Oleson remarking that Charles is "the richest man in Walnut Grove."

The two-part "Remember Me," broadcast on November 5 and 12, is justifiably regarded by many *Little House* fans to be one of the best, if not *the* best, episodes of the entire series. Landon wrote the script specifically with legendary Patricia Neal (winner of the Best Actress Academy Award for 1963's *Hud*) in mind. Neal, who had suffered a number of strokes since 1965 and was recovering from the latest one, politely declined the role, but Landon, unable to envision anyone else for the part, told her he would wait until she was well. Every member of the *Little House* cast and crew—from Landon on down—shared the same austere dressing facilities on location, as did all guest stars. Neal, however, was given her own Winnebago trailer to make the shoot as comfortable as possible. Although she had to sometimes rely on a teleprompter to recite her lines, the veteran actress gives a performance as honest and affecting as any ever seen on network television.

"Remember Me" starts with an older dog being separated from

her three newborn puppies, symbolic of the story ahead. (The shot of the whimpering mother watching as a wagon carries away her newborns is guaranteed to break the heart of any animal lover, which Landon, the owner of many pets over the years, had to know.) The Ingalls girls rescue the dogs from a potentially watery grave, and on the advice of their parents decide to see if any of their schoolmates might be interested in adopting the animals. Laura vows that she will not tell Nellie Oleson because "she won't really love it." Widow Julia Sanderson (Patricia Neal) stops by the Ingalls farm with her three children (John, Carl and Alicia) to ask Charles if he will do the harrowing at her place, followed by Isaiah and another Walnut Grove widow, Grace Snyder (Bonnie Bartlett), the local postal worker whom Isaiah has been courting. (Charles and Isaiah go to Sleepy Eye on business, freeing Landon to temporarily concentrate solely on his directorial duties.) The three women accompany the children to town, and on the way the Sanders boys con their sister into asking their mother if they can have one of the puppies. Julia gives her consent in a lighthearted scene that contrasts dramatically with the next sequence: Doc Baker confirms that she has lymphoma. She asks how soon she can expect to die. Baker, who cannot bring himself to face her, admits that he does not know exactly. All she says is, "I'll be darned" and—after a few seconds of silence—"Thank you, doctor." Julia leaves, the bell on the door ringing while the camera stays on Baker standing dejectedly in his office. When Julia returns to her farm she finds Charles working in the field, and with her back to him announces simply that she is going to die, adding that it is "a heck of a thing to tell a neighbor." Seeing the tears beginning to well up in Charles' eyes, she says she needs help finding families for her children, not sympathy. He tells her he will ask the church congregation on Sunday, but she replies that she will, asking him only to promise that he will make sure the children stay together. Charles agrees. Turning toward the house and forcing a smile, Julia says she intends to make a special supper that night and have a talk with her children. An impressive long shot accompanied by David Rose's beautiful score captures her as she strides across the dusty field to be reunited with the children, who are playing with the puppy and react joyfully at the sight of their mother. As expected, the news that she is dying does not go over well, regardless of how positively Julia attempts to present it. John, the oldest of the Sanderson offspring, begins to sob. Julia reprimands him, saying he is crying for himself, not for her. She puts on a good front, but looks worried and weary afterward. In church, Julia lines the children up in front of the congregation and breaks the news, implying that she wants them kept together. There is silence in the church after the Sandersons are gone. Reverend Alden speaks briefly, and the people wordlessly file outdoors. Landon cleverly changes the somber tone by having Julia ask where the Sunday picnic is going to be. At the picnic, the children—except for Laura—frolic with Charles and Isaiah. Julia asks Caroline and Grace to join in the fun, telling them she wants her children "to remember me laughing." When she invites Laura to play, Laura says she prefers to watch out for ants. Later, Laura admits to her father that she is afraid to be near Julia because the woman is going to die. Charles replies, "You can't spend your whole life worrying about dying. That's the way you live this life, each day, one at a time. Now, if you spend your whole life worrying about something that's going to happen, before you know it your life's over and you spent an awful lot of it just worrying. Now that's what life's all about—laughing and loving each other. And knowing that people aren't really gone when they die. We have all the good memories to sustain us 'til we see them again." The affirmative mood of this sequence is juxtaposed against the scene in which Doc Baker comes to the Ingalls house on a rainy night to report that Julia has collapsed and wants to see Charles and Caroline. Julia gives Reverend Alden a note to read at her funeral. "Read it loud and clear so everyone can hear," she instructs him. "Loud and clear," he replies. "You'll hear me." She reminds Charles of his promise and tells him Grace will take care of the children until he makes his decision. Julia listens to the rain falling outside and remarks that it ought to be a good year for the crops. With the children sitting on their mother's bed, the camera pulls back as the rain washes down the window pane, cutting to the rain falling on Julia's funeral. An overhead shot pans slowly in and down as Alden recites a passage of scripture, stopping on a close-up of his hands as he opens an envelope and reads the most poetic piece of writing Landon ever composed: "Remember me with smiles and laughter, for that is how I will remember you all. If you can only remember me with tears, then don't remember me at all." Alden tucks Julia's note into his Bible, looks up and says, "Loud and clear."

The second half of "Remember Me" is somewhat predictable but poignant, thanks largely to Landon's skill as a storyteller, as well as one of the most notable performances of Victor French's career. As expected in a rural community as economically strapped as Walnut Grove, Charles has no luck placing the Sanderson children in one home. A farmer is willing to take John and Carl, and Minerva Farnsworth, a wealthy cousin of Harriet Oleson, wants to adopt Alicia. Frustrated by the prospect of breaking his word to Julia, Charles tells Caroline that for the first time in his life he wishes he was rich. In the meantime, Isaiah and Grace have been bonding with the children. At another picnic, Isaiah ignores Minerva before lecturing her that there are more important things to give a child than money and a big house. He accuses Charles of doing the wrong thing, and confesses that he has been terribly lonely since losing his wife and daughter. When Minerva tells Charles she has decided to adopt Alicia, Charles asks her to make sure she loves the little girl. After visiting Julia's grave, he has the sad task of informing the Sandersons of his decision. John replies that his mother told them to do whatever Charles says, and that they know he did his best. Before leaving, Charles tells Isaiah and Grace that the children will be leaving after the church service on Thanksgiving. Nellie breaks the news about Minerva and Alicia to the Ingalls girls, and Laura reacts by angrily informing Charles that she is giving the remaining puppy to Nellie, adding that even though the dog will not be loved it will at least have a home—any home, just like Alicia. Finding Laura and the puppy alone, Caroline attempts to console her daughter by telling her what a hard decision Charles had to make, that he made the best decision he could for the Sandersons' future. She also says the Sandersons were more worried about Charles than themselves. Realizing her mother is right when she says Charles needs his family's love, not anger, Laura races to where her father is plowing, captured perfectly in another of Landon's long shots, no dialogue or close ups necessary. In church, however, there is a close shot of Alicia's hand taking Isaiah's as Reverend Alden prays. Outside, Isaiah agonizes as he watches the Sandersons say goodbye to each other, finally asking Grace—whom he has called "quite a woman"—to marry him. The story concludes effectively with a voice-over of Patricia Neal reciting the graveside poem as Landon freezes on a close up of Alicia's smiling face. Both David Rose and Ted Voigtlander received Emmy nominations for their work on "Remember Me," and an NBC publicist later referred to the episode as "a landmark." It is.

"At the End of the Rainbow" (12-1-75), written by Arthur Heinemann, was a decidedly more lighthearted episode in which Laura believes she has found gold at the bottom of Plum Creek. Director Landon imbues the proceedings with slightly diffused fantasy sequences as Laura daydreams of her family as the richest in town, renamed Ingalls Grove. In her reveries, they dress in white, live in a castle, and ride in an elegant carriage stuffed with candy and parcels. What the carriage cannot hold is carried by the Olesons, all dressed in rags. Back in the world of reality, a simple but imaginative tracking shot shows Charles arriving in Walnut Grove from inside the bank.

Landon wrote and directed "His Father's Son" (01-07-76), an exploration of Isaiah's attempt to bond with John, his newly-adopted eldest son, on a hunting trip. Of course the rugged outdoorsman and the aspiring writer have little in common. Isaiah is excited to give John a Winchester 73 rifle for his birthday, but does not understand the young man's aversion to killing. John tries to explain his feelings by writing Isaiah a note, not realizing his father cannot read. Even when a bear attacks Isaiah, John cannot bring himself to shoot, instead running to get help. (Landon shows French in a close shot during the attack—no need to substitute an actor wearing a phony bear costume.) Charles becomes involved in the dilemma between father and son, assuring John there is nothing wrong with him, that Isaiah is concerned about his wellbeing, and that Isaiah does not know how to read. Isaiah apologizes to John for not showing him what a good hunter he is; John reads the note, apologizing for not being the kind of son Isaiah wants. They embrace, and Isaiah calls John "son." Landon neatly bookends the episode by opening on John reading in the tree house Isaiah constructed for the boys in "Remember Me," and closing on a shot of Isaiah inside the tree house studying a beginning reader.

Writer/producer John Hawkins wrote "The Long Road Home"

(03-03-76), a change of pace adventure directed by Landon that concerns Charles and Isaiah's hauling explosives for the railroad when a bumper crop devalues the worth of their grain. The men conveniently "forget" to tell their wives about the risk of moving wagons filled with nitroglycerin, Caroline and Grace learning what their husbands are up to only when receiving $5,000 insurance policies in the mail. Working outdoors on a remote location with an all-male cast of former *Bonanza* guest stars (Richard Jaeckel, Lou Gossett, Bill Quinn, Larry Golden, Robert Doyle, Jim Mitchum), Landon may have felt as though he were back on his old series.

The second season ended with "Going Home" (03-31-76), a well-constructed story written and directed by Landon. After a tornado hits the Ingalls farm, ruining the crops, killing livestock and damaging the house, Charles interprets this as God telling him to take the family back to Wisconsin. Isaiah and Lars Hansen try to talk him out of it, but he will not listen. Laura begs him to reconsider leaving Walnut Grove, insisting that the family can make it if they all pull together. Her pleas do no good, so she confides in Reverend Alden, who tells her God does not protect all good folks from misfortune, but provides strength to get through difficult times. Laura says that for the first time her father looks old. She and Alden pray, the camera moving in on their hands. Matthew and Anna Simms, an elderly couple who owned the Ingalls homestead forty years before, offer to buy it if Charles will help repair the house. He agrees, but later changes his mind, asking Caroline what has happened to him, why has he let his family down by selfishly deciding to leave Walnut Grove without considering their feelings. Caroline proposes they stay and start over, even if it means having to build a new house with a dirt floor. Matthew Simms realizes Charles is making the same mistake he did forty years ago, and Anna admits she will be happy anywhere as long as they are together. When Charles asks if the family can stay on the property until they find a new place, Matthew says the deal is off because he is now too old for farming, that Charles can pay him for helping with repairs by making a donation to the church. Sitting in their wagon on the rise above the farm, Matthew and Anna watch as the Ingalls family gathers outside the house, then slowly ride on. The episode is filled with striking visuals conceived by Landon, including that of animals eating quietly at night before the coming storm causes the barn door to suddenly blast open. The devastation of the Ingalls farm unfolds from a shot of a dead chicken, and another of the family emerging from the sod house, to Charles discovering a hole in the barn roof and the body of a dead calf. The already compelling story is further enriched by the budding romance of Mary Ingalls and John Sanderson, which Landon depicts in two touchingly awkward yet sensitive scenes which give the viewer a hint of developments to come.

Little House and *The Waltons*, the series to which the Ingalls saga was most compared, tied at #15 in the year-end ratings for the 1976-77 season. It was an exceptionally busy time for Landon, who wrote and directed three episodes, directed five others, and finally saw the realization of a long-gestating pet project that NBC had been turning down for three years. The third season of his series kicked off with writer Arthur Heinemann's "The Collection" (09-27-76), a strong Landon-directed segment guest starring country legends Johnny and June Carter Cash as Caleb and Mattie Hodgekiss. While Mattie tends to an injured Reverend Alden, Caleb, a con artist, goes to Walnut Grove posing as a minister and friend of Alden. According to Caleb, he has to take what he can when he can because that is the way the world is, but promises Mattie that fleecing the town will be his last criminal act. In the process of trying to take advantage of various citizens, Caleb actually provides assistance, and ends up being applauded by the church congregation. In the scene where Caleb comforts little Alicia Edwards after the death of her puppy, Landon frames the entire conversation in a close shot of the two characters. Later, when Caleb lets himself into Oleson's Mercantile at night, the action is shown from the Oleson's dog's point of view.

Landon wrote and directed the following week's episode, "Bunny" (10-04-76), which opens with a long shot of Laura running across a field, then moves in on an apple that she plucks off the tree for Bunny, a horse she once owned but traded to the Oleson's in exchange for a stove for Caroline. After school, Nellie, astride Bunny, whips Laura and Mary with a riding crop. The horse bolts, and Nellie is knocked out of the saddle by a tree branch. Although Doc Baker says the girl has only a slight concussion, Nellie claims she cannot feel her legs, prompting Harriet to insist that Bunny be destroyed. With Nels Oleson's blessing, Laura hides the horse at the Ingalls farm. Nellie asks Laura to help with their homework assignments every day so she will not fall behind in her studies while her legs try to mend. Consequently, Laura's own schoolwork suffers, and her problems only mount when Harriet discovers that Bunny has not run away. Discovering that Nellie is not paralyzed, Laura takes her nemesis, sitting in the wheelchair Charles has refurbished, to the top of a hill and sends the chair and its occupant on a wild ride back down. Nellie lands in the mill pond, coming up covered in slime. Seeing that her daughter is no longer an invalid, Harriet faints. Nels gives Bunny back to Laura, telling her that an animal is no different from a person—it has to be with someone who loves it. Nellie catches sight of Laura riding away with a boy she likes and throws a tantrum, breaking all the things Harriet got for her while "crippled." (Landon's "Bunny" has become a favorite episode among *Little House* fans. An entertaining account of its filming is given in Alison Arngrim's book.)

"Little Girl Lost" (10-18-76) was written by Paul W. Cooper and directed by Landon. When Carrie Ingalls falls into the ventilation shaft of an abandoned coal mine her only hope is Wendell Loudy (veteran actor John Ireland), a former mining engineer who is now the town drunk. Complicating efforts to rescue the girl is normally amiable mill owner Lars Hansen. Hansen holds Loudy responsible for the death of a woman he cared for twenty years ago, and now will neither give Loudy a job nor believe anything the man suggests to save Carrie. In the scene where Hansen tells Charles why he hates Loudy, Landon concentrates on a medium close shot of Hansen, with Charles standing behind him in the shadows. Also typical of Landon, the rescue attempts are filmed in darkness with minimal but effective lighting that emphasizes the actions of the actors.

Landon the actor shines prominently in the two-part "Journey in the Spring," (November 15 and 22), which he also wrote and directed. After Charles receives a letter informing him that his mother has died he returns to Wisconsin intent on bringing his father back with him. His father, Lansford Ingalls (Arthur Hill), dwells only on his failures and has given up on life. He is reluctant to leave with Charles, but finally relents. At the Ingalls farm, Lansford chooses to live in the sod house, saying he and Charles do not really know each other anymore and it would feel strange living under the same roof. Although Lansford bonds with Laura, who is named after Charles' late mother, their relationship falls apart when her horse is fatally injured but Lansford assures her the animal can be saved. Charles, angry at his father for giving Laura false hope, puts the horse out of its misery. (Landon films Laura fleeing from the site and stopping abruptly at the sound of Charles' rifle before continuing to run.) Isaiah Edwards convinces Laura to make up with her grandfather, telling her there is no one to blame, that some things just happen and there is no way to keep all promises, especially to loved ones. Lansford, however, has left to try going back to Wisconsin on a train. Laura goes after him, followed by Charles and Isaiah. In a voice-over, Laura reveals that her grandfather stayed through the winter but had to leave in the spring to be near his late wife. Landon enhances this fairly straightforward story with an amusing subplot involving Carrie and the Ingalls' Thanksgiving turkey, flashbacks to Charles' days as a young boy (played by future series regular Matthew Laborteaux), and numerous emotional scenes, all impressively staged: The impending death of Charles' mother is implied by having her ask how long until sunup while the light is already streaming into the cabin. Lansford's fragile state is obvious when he mistakenly believes the adult Charles is still a boy. Charles accuses his father of always being depressed and bringing everyone down, adding that Lansford has wasted his life feeling sorry for himself. After Lansford slaps him, Charles says he is glad his mother is not there to see him, that all she ever wanted was for her husband to be happy. In a flashback to their younger days, Charles' mother tells him not to be afraid to dream or fail because if he is brave but still fails it will only make him stronger. The scene ends with a flower—one of Landon's favorite symbols—floating on water, a reprise of similar visual images seen in *Bonanza*'s "Love Child," the previous season's "Remember Me," and more to come, including this episode's conclusion: As Lansford disappears into the woods, the camera moves in on a daisy before the fadeout.

On the night of December 20, 1976, NBC's entire primetime schedule was devoted to Michael Landon, leading with a special 90-minute installment of *Little House* and concluding with the television movie he had been pressuring the network to allow him to make since the end of *Bonanza*. The expanded episode, writer Harold Swanton's "The Hunters," was directed by Landon and featured rare guest appearances by Burl Ives, *The Rifleman*'s Johnny Crawford, and *Rawhide*'s Paul Brinegar. (Knowledgeable viewers could also recognize familiar music by David Rose heard as far back as 1959 in "The Newcomers," the second episode of *Bonanza*.) Charles takes Laura along on a hunting trip to the high country, and on their second day out they come across father and son trappers Sam (Ives) and Ben (Crawford) Shelby. Sam is blind and has not been more than one hundred feet from their cabin in five years. Charles and Laura move on but are forced to make a treacherous trek back to the Shelby cabin after Laura accidentally causes Charles to be shot and their horse is killed in a fall. They find Sam there alone, and the blind man and Laura go off in search of Ben. When another trapper (Brinegar) arrives at the cabin, he misses seeing Charles, who has gone outside and fallen down looking for water. Landon expertly elevates a potentially monotonous tale with logical pacing, believable doses of suspense, and his usual creative use of beautiful outdoor settings.

"The Loneliest Runner" (12-20-76)

In November 1976, Landon was able to produce *The Loneliest Runner*, a semi-autobiographical television film about bedwetting that he had been trying to convince NBC to let him do since 1973. "There are 20 million bed-wetters in this country," he said before his project was given the go-ahead. "Out of the network executives who turn off when you mention the subject, two out of five were bed-wetters themselves." As a young boy, Landon himself had endured the stigma of bedwetting, a situation made only worse by his clueless parents. To humiliate him, his mother would hang his soiled bed sheets out the window for the neighborhood to see. "I had to sleep all curled up in a baby bed because my mother wouldn't buy a new bed until I got over the bedwetting," he revealed. In the course of doing research, Landon learned that bedwetting is caused by a deep-sleep pattern and can be inherited. "A year before my father died, he confessed that he had had the same problem as a youth. If only he had told me earlier, it would have saved me tremendous suffering and shame."

When released on home video in 1990, *The Loneliest Runner* was advertised as "an uplifting story of a boy's growth into manhood" and illustrated by a photo of Landon as the title character (John Curtis) running in the Olympics, which is how the film opens. The entire story is a flashback to the events that inspired Curtis (Lance Kerwin) to become interested in running. He has been promised a full-size bed for his thirteenth birthday and lies to his parents, assuring them he has been dry for five nights. As an excuse to stop by the Laundromat to wash his wet sheets before going to school, John says he has early football practice. One morning he finds the laundry closed, and when his father (Brian Keith, on whose 1955-56 series *Crusader* Landon guest starred) drives him and two friends home after a game, John is humiliated to see that his mother has hung his soiled sheet outside his bedroom window. His mother, Alice (another use of Landon's favored female name), says he is "too damn lazy" to get up and use the toilet. John has to resort to a series of lies and contrivances to deal with the complications caused by his condition, racing home after school every day to pull his sheets from public display. As a result, in gym class he, a ninth grader, beats the senior record for the half-mile run. A coach tells him it is possible for him to become a great varsity runner if he practices for an hour after school every day, but the news does not impress Alice (DeAnn Mears). She accepts an invitation to an overnight get-together for him, saying she wants to see if he also wets the bed away from home. At the sleepover John forces himself to stay awake all night and remain dry. Inevitably, he has another nocturnal accident, only this time he does not succeed in making it home before a girl he likes sees the sheet hanging out the window. Deeply ashamed, he hides out in a department store after hours and falls asleep on an adult bed. The store calls his parents, and when they arrive, John excitedly tells them he really had a dry night, that he knew his problem would disappear as soon as he saw the full-size mattresses. His father confesses that he had the same trouble as a boy and apologizes. Alice, who has dismissed a doctor's diagnosis of bedwetting being hereditary, rambles on while father and son talk until her husband tells her to shut up. A shot of the coach's stopwatch segues neatly to a clock in a television studio where the adult John Curtis (Landon) is being interviewed by Rafer Johnson about winning the 26-mile Olympic Marathon. When asked how and why he could run like that, John replies that he owes his achievement to his mother and father. The film ends with the camera freezing on Landon as he breaks the tape at the finish line. To imaginatively establish the time and place of *The Loneliest Runner*, Landon shows an issue of the *Los Angeles Chronicle* and a broadcast of television's *Name That Tune*—with a sly snippet of David Rose's famous "Holiday for Strings"—instead of relying solely on the outdated look of fashion and vehicles. The exact year is pinpointed later in a shot where the calendar changes from 1955 to 1956, a device that lazy screenwriters often employ to inform viewers; Landon uses it after the general period has been suggested, and only to illustrate the passage of time. In addition to Brian Keith, Landon and Susan McCray cast such familiar faces as Bing Russell (*Bonanza*'s Deputy Clem Foster) as a gym teacher, and *Little House*'s Melissa Sue Anderson as John's neighbor, Nancy.

If some network executives continued to be squeamish about the subject matter of *The Loneliest Runner*—which critic Leonard Maltin called a "sensitive drama"—they had to be pleased when the film proved to be a ratings success. Landon reportedly received a flood of mail from viewers who had endured the stigma of bedwetting and appreciated his courage in bringing the condition to light so publicly.

* * *

Back on the prairie, Landon directed a Robert Janes script entitled "The Music Box" (03-14-77). As in "Bunny," Laura is manipulated by Nellie, but this time she is fully aware of the circumstances. Offended by Nellie's ridiculing of a classmate, Anna, who stutters, Laura steals a music box from Nellie and hides it in the hayloft of the Ingalls barn. When Nellie finds out what Laura has done, she says she will not tell anyone if Laura agrees to join her secret club, an organization that does not include Anna. At first, Laura reluctantly goes along with Nellie's mistreatment of Anna before eventually doing the right thing by confessing to stealing the music box.

Landon's imagination as a filmmaker is on full display, opening with the camera panning across an assortment of wares in Olesen's store, to an upside down shot from Laura's point-of-view in the barn. Laura's guilty conscience inspires an amusing trio of slightly surreal dream sequences.

Landon wrapped up the third season with "Gold Country" (04-04-77), a two-hour installment written by John Hawkins and B.W. Sandefur that finds the Ingalls and Edwards families traveling 400 miles to the gold fields of South Dakota after constant rainfall makes it impossible for them to plant their crops. Filmed in and around Arizona's Old Tucson movie location, a site very familiar to Landon from the later years of *Bonanza*, the episode is one of the few times *Little House* came close to resembling a classic television Western. As always, Landon makes good use of shooting the wide open spaces as well as several key moments of drama: Isaiah is beaten and robbed outside a saloon, a prospector is shot for not revealing where he has hidden his gold, Isaiah wields a shotgun to ward off a pair of claim jumpers, an elderly prospector blames Laura for disclosing the location of his gold. In the end, Charles lectures the church congregation about real wealth not being gold, and the Ingalls family returns to Walnut Grove. As for the Edwards clan…

The fourth season of *Little House* began with a new family in the community, and no mention of what had happened to Isaiah, Grace, and their three adopted children. For many fans, the saga of the residents of Walnut Grove, in retrospect, peaked during the third year, due in large part to such top grade episodes as "The Collector," "Bunny," "Journey in the Spring," "The Hunters," "Gold Country," and several others not written or directed by Landon ("Blizzard," "I'll Ride the Wind," "Quarantine," "To Live with Fear," "The Wisdom of Solomon"), but all of which benefited from his close supervision. Adding considerably to the appeal of the series was the presence of Victor French, who felt undervalued by NBC and lobbied unsuccessfully for a raise. ABC, however, was only too glad to cash in on his new-found popularity and offered him the lead role as Southern lawman Roy Mobey in *Carter Country*, a sitcom set in Georgia. French accepted, and according to *Little House* producer Kent McCray, "Michael felt he'd lost a brother, a member of his very tight group on the show. Michael always looked to Victor to hash out problems in a script or on the set. And then Victor was gone, and it hurt." Even though it lasted for two seasons, *Carter Country* was never a big hit.

Despite the absence of French, the fourth year of *Little House on the Prairie* was the highest-rated in its history, ranking #7 at the end of the season and NBC's only show in the top ten. When asked how long he felt the series would last, Landon said, "I have no idea. If everybody is having fun making the show, that's great. If we had the same competition every year, I could tell you how many years we'd be on. If you're eating up the competition and they're not going to change it, then you're going to be on quite a while. But they change the competition every year." *Little House*'s competition at the beginning of the 1977-78 season was *The San Pedro Beach Bums*, an hour-long sitcom on ABC, and *Young Dan'l Boone* on CBS, neither of which made it to the end of the 1977.

To replace the Edwards family, Landon created the Garveys, introduced in the fourth season's debut episode, "Castoffs." In the role of patriarch Jonathan Garvey was former Los Angeles Rams defensive tackle Merlin Olsen, whose fifteen-year football career ended in 1976. Landon was reminded of Dan Blocker while viewing film of Olsen's audition for the part, and confessed to becoming teary-eyed. "There was a surface resemblance," he said, "but what I saw in Merlin, big and gentle like Dan, was his own essential honesty. He doesn't push or strain, he listens and he opens up the emotions." Olsen admitted that as an actor he had to work on "how to release emotions I had to learn to control as an athlete. On the field, emotions like fear and anger are useful only to a limited degree. Playing a role, I've found it easier to deal with compassion than with anger. It's very hard for me to portray honest anger…I am simply not an angry man." Unlike some athletes who attempted an acting career, Olsen possessed a natural ability that justified Landon's instincts, and he remained on the series into its seventh season. Cast as Alice (that name again!) Garvey was Hersha Parady, who had portrayed Caroline Ingalls' sister-in-law in the previous season's "Journey in the Spring." The Garvey's son, Andy, was played by Patrick Laborteaux, whose brother, Matthew, had appeared briefly as young Charles Ingalls in "Journey in the Spring" and would later become a series regular.

The Garveys were introduced in "Castoffs" (09-12-77), the fourth season premiere, written by Tony Kayden and directed by Landon, who would direct ten episodes during the coming year. The title refers not only to Bandit, the new dog in the Ingalls' life, but also Kezia Horn (Hermione Baddeley), an odd newcomer to Walnut Grove. Sadly, Laura finds her faithful dog, Jack, dead in the barn. Charles tells her Jack was old and tired, that his time had come, and they can bury him on the hill where he liked to play. Landon captures this touching moment in a beautiful long shot of the family standing on the hill, clouds overhead. Bandit, a stray dog that follows Charles home from a freight run to Mankato, is first rejected by Laura and has to work at winning her heart. Similarly, eccentric Kezia Horn, who chooses to live in a burned out house with a pet crow and a horse that eats beef jerky, is shunned by most of the townspeople except for the children and kindly Jonathan Garvey.

"My Ellen" (09-26-77) the first of two episodes for the season written and directed by Landon, is also one of the darkest and disturbing to date. "Everyone said when the show went on the air that it was too soft," Landon said. "I told the network that with only seven people in Walnut Grove, if there were any fights it would be a ghost town. Family entertainment doesn't have to be sweetness and light. Compared to the tone of the books, I'm the Marquis de Sade." In "My Ellen," Eloise Taylor, a local farmwife, becomes mentally unbalanced after her daughter drowns, trapping Laura in a root cellar as a replacement for the dead girl. A childlike hermit named Busby is suspected of abducting Laura when one of her schoolbooks is found among his possessions. Laura manages to escape from Eloise, but not before Eloise's husband, Cal, has shot and wounded Busby. Busby explains that all he wanted to do was look at the pictures in the Laura's book, and she and Charles let him keep it. A couple of Landon's distinctive creative traits from past productions are echoed here: a nighttime search by torchlight, and a mother throwing herself on a child's coffin. The camera focuses on Eloise's face as a man's voice announces that the searchers have found Ellen's body, and when Busby is shot by Cal, the action is captured in a long shot from behind Cal's back, with Busby dropping in the distance.

Landon next directed John T. Dugan's "To Run and Hide," broadcast on Landon's forty-first birthday. Despondent after losing a patient, Doc Baker tells Charles he is going to retire and grow corn. Doctor Logan, Walnut Grove's new physician, proves to be an arrogant sort who will not treat anyone unable to pay him in cash. When the wife of the man Baker could not save experiences difficulty giving birth, Logan is off hunting, and it is up to Charles to convince Baker to step in. The delivery is a success, and Baker thanks Charles for talking sense to him.

"The High Price of Being Right" (11-14-77), written by Don Balluck and directed by Landon, focuses on the Garveys. Disaster strikes in the form of a fire that burns the entire crop Jonathan has harvested, and he is too proud and stubborn to accept charity or allow Alice to take a job in the local post office. Divorce seems to be inevitable until the very end of the episode, a domestic drama enriched not only by skillful acting, but Landon's directorial touches as well, beginning with a close up of Jonathan's hands, folded in a prayer of thanks for a good crop and a loving family. The camera starts on a fire burning in the fireplace, then follows a shower of sparks as they move upward, out the chimney and blowing into straw on the barn floor.

A dynamic performance by the late Moses Gunn, who joins the series as Joe Kagan, is the highlight of "The Fighter" (11-21-77), a 90-minute episode directed by Landon from a teleplay he based on a story by Lawrence M. Connor. Fourteen years after being badly beaten in a prizefight and abandoned by his wife and son, Joe and his crooked manager, Moody (Raymond St. Jacques), arrive in Walnut Grove offering fifty dollars to anyone who can stay in the ring with Joe for three minutes. Doctors have told Joe he is no longer in any condition to fight, but as he told his wife years before, "I have to! It's what I do! It's all I can do!" Jonathan signs up to fight Joe, but injures his hand and asks Charles to take his place. Charles succeeds in knocking Joe out, but decides to give him the prize money when Doc Baker discovers the shape Joe is in. When the old fighter tries to hang himself, Charles feels obligated to take care of him. Later, Charles accompanies Joe to Springfield (the Old Tucson set) to sign papers giving Joe possession of a farm near Walnut Grove. There, Joe discovers that his son, Tim, is being promoted as a fighter by

Moody, and overhears Tim telling reporters that his father is dead. Joe accuses Moody of stealing from him, tells him to stay away from Tim, and that he is fighting the young man himself. Tim is knocked out by Joe and decides to work in his aunt's store in Denver, never learning Joe's identity. "The Fighter" earned Emmys for cinematographer Ted Voigtlander and makeup artists Hank Edds and Allan Snyder.

"Freedom Flight" (12-12-77), written by Ron Chinquy and directed by Landon, is, like "Gold Country," a return to the flavor of the Old West. Defying the more bigoted citizens of Walnut Grove, Charles gives sanctuary to an elderly Indian chief who has suffered a stroke. The chief and his people have abandoned a worthless reservation and are trying to return to their rightful land, and with the help of Charles and Doc Baker they succeed. Once again, director Landon makes excellent use of the vast expanse of the prairie as the Indians outrun their pursuers, including soldiers armed with a Gatling gun.

In "Whisper Country" (01-16-78), written by John Hawkins and directed by Landon, Mary Ingalls takes a teaching job in a strange rural community forty miles from Walnut Grove. Her struggle to establish herself and fit in is complicated by Rachel Peel, a woman who values religion over education. Peel is exposed as a bigot and a fraud, and Landon punctuates the uplifting conclusion with a close shot of Mary and Rachel's hands in a friendly clasp.

In an era when television was rapidly favoring style over substance, with an emphasis on getting shows done quickly rather than taking time to write and shoot creatively, the superiority of a Michael Landon production was glaringly obvious. A prime example is "Be My Friend" (01-30-78), another 90-minute episode and Landon's final effort of the season as both writer and director. The premise is basically simple: A lonely young woman gives birth out of wedlock and deliberately leaves the baby for Laura to find. As always, Landon's characters are well-drawn, the story itself consistently engaging, with moments of pathos and humor. The unmarried woman, Anna, is the daughter of Nathaniel Mears, a single father, a judgmental zealot whose wife was allegedly evil. Anna gives birth in secret, her only connection to the world outside her forest home the messages she puts in bottles and tosses into the creek. Laura finds three of these bottles with their touching contents: "If you find this, be my friend." "Dear Friend, if you find this, my eyes are brown and this is my hair. Be my friend." The final message—"This is me. Be my friend" is accompanied by a photograph. Charles and Laura eventually search for the source of the bottles and come across Anna's crying infant in a basket with a note reading, "Please be my friend. Please love me." They take the baby, a girl Laura names Grace, to Doc Baker, who declares the child healthy, but warns that girls are not easy to adopt out. (As an amusing aside, Charles tells busybody Harriet Oleson that the baby is Laura's, and when Harriet spots Laura with her son Willie she screams, assuming he is the father.) Charles travels to Boswell (Paramount's Western set) and learns that the baby's mother is Anna Mears, daughter of an unfriendly man who moved away so Anna could not be with Bobby Harris, the boy who wanted to marry her. Anna and Bobby are reunited, but not before Nathaniel attempts to burn down his cabin with him and Anna inside. While Bobby, Anna and their baby go off to begin a new life, the ending is not altogether positive, Landon tempering it by keeping Nathaniel bitter and mean-spirited.

Landon went behind the camera for Arthur Heinemann's "The Stranger" (02-20-78), filmed partly at Golden Oak Ranch, a location used extensively by *Bonanza*. Unable to have any influence on Peter Landstrom, a bratty young relative whose father has sent him to Walnut Grove to benefit from a "frontier upbringing," the Olesens turn him over to Charles. Naturally, the boy is turned around by the good examples set by the Ingalls family.

Golden Oak Ranch was used again in "A Most Precious Gift" (11-27-78), written by Carole and Michael Raschella, and Landon's tenth and final directorial duty of the season. Charles and Caroline add a fourth daughter to their brood, with verbal and visual references back to "The Lord is My Shepherd," in which their baby son died. The imminent birth of the new child, named Grace, is hinted at in the episode's first scene, the camera moving in to show eggs in a bird's nest.

The season ended with the memorable and emotional two-part episode "I'll Be Waving as You Drive Away," which resulted in an Emmy nomination for Melissa Sue Anderson. Mary Ingalls loses her sight and moves to a school for the blind, where she meets her future husband, Adam Kendall (Linwood Boomer), a development that came as no surprise to readers of the original books. Landon mentioned it to the press shortly after production of the fourth year had begun, adding, "The girls on the show are growing up, and the concept wouldn't work having them remain at home when they're getting older. You can't get away with things like we did on *Bonanza*, with guys in their thirties living with Pa. Audiences just won't buy it." He also disclosed that if the series was granted a fifth season the Ingalls family would sell their farm and move to a larger town, where Charles and Caroline would manage a boarding house. Newest regular cast member Boomer was relatively new to acting and nervous about his first major role being that of a blind person, but Landon put him at ease. "Michael is terrific," Boomer said. "The first day on location I walked into his dressing room expecting to find a lavish suite, and it was just a little room with bugs. He smiled and said, 'You like the way the stars live, kid?'"

Although it dipped to #14 in the annual ratings, the fifth season of *Little House* was NBC's sole program in the top twenty. It was a season of change, with Walnut Grove once again falling on hard times and the Ingalls pulling up stakes and moving to Winoka in "As Long as We're Together" (September 11 and 18), a two-part installment written and directed by Landon. For anyone who has had to move reluctantly, the scene where Charles and Caroline reminisce in their empty home is tough to watch. In Winoka they get jobs at a hotel called the Dakota, Charles as manager, Caroline as cook. Laura meets a homeless boy named Albert (Matthew Laborteaux), who lives under a staircase survives by shining shoes and gambling. When the Garveys and the Olesons show up in Winoka, Alice Garvey starts a school, and Jonathan gets a job as a bouncer in the saloon where both Nels and Harriet Oleson find employment. Director Landon makes good use of the show's new environment: the Winoka set at Paramount rarely reminds the viewer that it was once Virginia City during the first ten seasons of *Bonanza*, the chaotic scene where Charles chases Albert down the street is appropriately captured by a hand-held camera, Jonathan's hands are shown in a close up when they squeeze a miscreant in a bear hug, and the gathering for Mary's birthday party ends with an elevated long shot.

"The Man Inside" ((10-02-78), also written and directed by

Landon, opens with the camera panning around a room, from the stomach of John Bevins (Cliff Emmich), a sleeping fat man, to his large pants on a chair, and his oversize shoes. (When John and his wife, Bess, discuss his weight problem, there is a reference to a wormy apple, a favorite reference in Landon's writing.) John is the Winoka school's handyman and an embarrassment to his daughter, Amelia, who pretends she does not know him. To her mother, Laura tearfully confesses to laughing at John before she learned he is Amelia's father, and Caroline reminds her to never make unkind remarks about anyone. John makes light of his large girth, going along with jokes made at his expense, but is crushed when he overhears Amelia telling Bess she does not want anyone to know he is her father. He tells his wife and daughter he is leaving to work on the railroad, but really intends to hide out in the supply room of the blind school and work on repairing the roof at night. After being seriously injured in a fall, John does not want to be operated on and has no will to live. Charles tells Bess and Amelia that John is not working for the railroad and is badly in need of surgery. Bess begs her husband to let the doctor operate, but he says he is a freak, wants her and Amelia to have a better life without him, and that he does not want to ruin their lives. John passes out, and Bess tells the doctor to go ahead with the operation. Amelia hears a blind student read an essay praising John, then goes to sit beside his bed while he recuperates. Believing her father is asleep, she admits to hurting him and does not expect him to love her, but says he has to live for the many people who love him. She lays her head on his chest, and the camera moves in on John's hand as it reaches up to pat Amelia's head. "The Man Inside" is a prime example of Landon's belief in accepting those who may be different, and benefits from an excellent job by actor Emmich.

A mere five weeks after moving to Winoka, the expatriates from Walnut Grove contemplate going back to their hometown in the first part of "There's No Place Like Home" (10-09-78), written and directed by Landon. Mary decides to stay behind and teach at the blind school, telling Charles he has to do what is right for him for a change, not the whole family. She says she is happy doing what she loves, and that he cannot stay there and be unhappy simply for her sake. The episode introduces Ray Bolger, who achieved immortality as the Scarecrow in *The Wizard of Oz*, as shiftless dreamer Toby Noe, a role he would reprise before the season was over. The episode's second half (10-16-78) was also written by Landon, but directed by William F. Claxton. Charles and Caroline offer to take Albert home with them, and the boy replies that he will stay as long as he is needed, but that the situation will not be permanent. The children at the blind school give the Ingalls a horseshoe for good luck, which Charles nails over the doorway of the Little House. The Ingalls' property is in bad shape, as is the town of Walnut Grove, with weeds growing in the street and cobwebs filling the schoolhouse/ church. Nels says there is no money to hire a teacher, and no one attends church. Doc Baker is tending to Lars Hanson, felled by a stroke. This was the final appearance by aging actor Karl Swenson, who as Hanson rallies from his debilitated condition to climb the church steps unaided, the citizens of the town he founded fifty years before watching in admiration. As the congregation files inside, the camera pulls back to reveal a sign which reads, "Walnut Grove, Founded 1840 By Lars Hanson." In a voice-over, Laura says Lars died four months later. (Ironically, Karl Swenson passed away October 8, 1978, one day before the airing of Part One.)

"Fagin" (10-23-78), written by Carole and Michael Raschella and directed by Landon, explores the growing relationship between Charles and his young charge, Albert, who is considering a future in farming. In order to teach the boy about livestock, Charles gives him a calf, which Albert names Fagin. Laura becomes jealous of the time her father spends with his new "son," yet it is Albert who runs away, feeling he has come between Charles and "Half-Pint." He leaves a note saying farming is not for him, and that Laura can take care of Fagin. At the fair in Sleepy Eye, Fagin wins first place in livestock competition, and Albert, Charles and Laura have a tearful reunion. Landon stages several interesting scenes, ranging from a close up of Fagin's head as the episode begins, to the camera panning along the prostrate animal and stopping on Charles and Albert as Fagin lies sick in the Ingalls barn. When Fagin pulls through and the women come running out of the house, Landon places the camera low, with a rooster in the foreground, rather than simply showing the women crossing from the house to the barn. The scene where Charles finds Laura at the fishing hole and apologizes for neglecting her is effectively shown in a single long shot.

In "The Wedding" (11-06-78), Landon directs Arthur Heinemann's script concerning the inevitable marriage of Mary to Adam Kendall. Charles and Caroline return to Winoka for the ceremony, only to find their daughter worried that her blindness will prevent her from successfully raising any children she may have. When Charles, Caroline, Adam and Mary reminisce, Landon stages the scene in a darkened room and has the camera focus on Mary's troubled expression. The wedding features two close ups of hands—Mary handing a bouquet to her flower girl, Adam taking Mary's ring—and a freeze frame on Mary and Adam kissing.

Landon directed the 90-minute episode "The Godsister" (12-18-78), written by Don Balluck, and the only time both Greenbush twins appeared together on camera, one as Carrie Ingalls, the other as Carrie's imaginary friend, Alissa. Feeling lonely and bored after Charles and Jonathan leave for work stringing telephone line between Springfield and Sleepy Eye, Carrie dreams up a companion that looks just like her. The fantasy sequences—which include a giant spider—have a suitably gauzy look that contrasts well with the gritty scenes of Charles and Jonathan working their way across the wilderness.

Ted Voigtlander's camerawork and David Rose's composing for Paul Wolff's "The Craftsman" (01-08-79) again snared *Little House* a pair of Emmys. Typically, Landon's direction is dramatic in its simplicity, as though the episode is a stage play, with little need for editing or fancy photography. Like his idols John Ford and Orson Welles, he was an economical and judicious filmmaker who was able to "cut in the camera" rather than spend hours in post-production. The story of Albert's friendship with an elderly Jewish woodworker is told with sensitivity, yet takes some pointed and amusing jabs at anti-Semitism along the way. Landon begins by having the camera pan across tools and hand-carved wood, resting on a hand rubbing stain into the wood before cutting to a close up of an old man's tearful face. Similarly, the ending starts with the camera moving slowly downward with a tree in the foreground, stopping on two grave markers and then closing in on Albert's hands as he plants a seedling for a tree.

Paul Wolff also wrote "Dance with Me" (01-22-79), another 90-minute installment directed by Landon. Largely a showcase for Ray Bolger, returning as Toby Noe, and Eileen Heckart, this is a somewhat atypical *Little House*, the regular characters relegated to more or less supporting roles in a gentle, amusing courtship tale.

The series' executive story consultant, John T. Dugan, contributed "The Lake Kezia Monster" (02-12-79), which Landon directed largely at Golden Oak Ranch. Walnut Grove's resident eccentric (Hermione Baddeley, in her third and final appearance as Kezia Horn) loses her lakeside house when Harriet Oleson pays the back taxes. Inspired by Kezia's account of the fabled Loch Ness Monster, the children conspire to scare the Olesons off by constructing a monster of their own. Landon enlivens the proceedings with some serviceable nighttime scenes as well as underwater shots, a comparative rarity for the series.

The Garvey family loses their barn again in Don Balluck's "Barn Burner" (02-19-79), a strong tale of bigotry directed by Landon. Charles and Jonathan tell their fellow farmers that all of them have to stick together on the price of wheat so they will not have to sell their bumper crops short. Only the town's most unpleasant citizen, Judd Larrabee (veteran Western actor Donald "Red" Barry, making his sixth and final appearance on the show), does not agree. Larrabee has the largest crop and does not want to get the same price as Joe Kagan, simply because Joe is black, but reluctantly says he will go along with the others. When he reneges on his promise, Charles calls him a thief and a liar. Later, at the Garvey barn, an angry Larrabee knocks Andy out. The barn catches fire after Andy rides off in search of his folks, and Larrabee is jailed in the icehouse to await trial. Unrepentant, Larrabee tells his wife nothing would have happened if the town had not allowed Joe to settle in Walnut Grove. The jury finds Larrabee guilty of assault and battery, but cannot decide on the charge of barn burning. Joe, who is one of the jurors, tells the court that Larrabee is probably guilty of torching the barn, but reminds the judge that no one saw him do it. Giving Larrabee the benefit of the doubt, the judge orders him to pay Garvey the price of the lost wheat instead of sentencing him to prison. Landon ends the episode by showing Larrabee in the schoolhouse, saying he does need anybody. And indeed there is no one else there, not even his long suffering wife, who has vowed to leave him regardless of the trial's outcome.

As and actor and frequent director of *Little House*, as well as executive producer, it is remarkable that Landon was also able to contribute as many scripts as he did. "I do my best work in the morning," he said. "I always start with fifteen or sixteen or seventeen shows before the season begins. We have a vacation spot in Hawaii, and in five weeks there I can turn out four screenplays." The pace of producing a television series is nearly relentless, as is the demand for new material, which is why it is not surprising that Landon would occasionally recycle some of his old ideas to fit a new setting. Such was the case with "Someone Please Love Me" (03-05-79), a *Bonanza* script ("A Dream to Dream") from eleven years before that he adapted for *Little House*. He turned the director's chair over to William F. Claxton, presumably so he could concentrate on his performance as the only Ingalls featured in the story. As Hoss Cartwright had done in the original version, Charles helps reunite a family torn apart by a drunken father mourning the death of a son.

"The Odyssey" (03-19-79), written by Carole and Michael Raschella, gave Landon another opportunity to direct one of the numerous episodes of the season that were set far from Walnut Grove. When Dylan Whitaker, an artistically gifted classmate, learns he is dying from leukemia, Laura and Albert join him on his quest to see the Pacific Ocean before he dies. Charles tells the boy's mother he will go after them, and ends up sharing a railroad boxcar with the runaways. Charles tells Dylan he is crazy to attempt such a journey, but Dylan says he does not want his mother to watch him die. In San Francisco they hitch a ride to the ocean with a wealthy newspaperman who pays Charles for Dylan's story, enabling them to afford the trip back to Minnesota. The story begins with the camera pulling back from a waterfall to Dylan painting the ocean, and ends with him running into the surf in slow motion, the camera pulling back as he stops and raises his arms in triumph. At one point during the episode, Laura asks Charles what he would do if he had only one month to live. Perhaps echoing Landon's actual feelings, Charles replies that he would want to live long enough to see his children grown, with families of their own.

As NBC's top-rated program, there was never any doubt that *Little House on the Prairie* would be renewed for the 1979-80 season, and in the year-end rankings it was one of only four shows on the network that managed to place in the top thirty, though it dropped from #14 to #16. Landon continued to distinguish himself as perhaps the most prolific person working in television, writing and directing thirteen of the twenty-three episodes and directing another five. Production of the series moved from Paramount to Metro-Goldwyn-Mayer Studios in Culver City, the interior sets taking over an entire massive soundstage.

Season Six began with Landon's "Back to School" (also known as "Laura's Love Story"), a two-part episode airing September 17 and 24. Introduced as Walnut Grove's newest residents are Eliza Jane Wilder (Lucy Lee Flippen), the new schoolteacher, and her brother, Almonzo (Dean Butler), Laura's future husband. A 900-pound millstone breaks loose from a wagon and breaks Charles' arm and some of his ribs, freeing Landon to go behind the camera for most of the proceedings, which includes the Olesons giving Nellie her own restaurant as a graduation gift, and Laura's growing pains. Most of the humor is provided by Nellie and Laura's competition for Almonzo's attention in what is essentially a trauma-less episode enhanced by Landon's imaginative eye: Laura carving her and Almonzo's initials in a tree, a long shot tracking of a wagon moving through a field of flowers, Charles and Laura conversing in front of the fireplace, a final close up of the initials Laura carved.

In John T. Dugan's teleplay "The Third Miracle" (10-08-79), based on a story by Kenneth Hunter, Charles is said to be in Mankato, once again allowing Landon to work his magic behind the scenes for at least part of the episode. A close up of a huge swarm of bees on a log next to Plum Creek is a prelude to Laura and Albert's discussion of what they intend to do with the money they receive once they have collected the hive's honey. They sell their bounty to Harriet Oleson and use the money to fund Adam and Mary's trip to St. Paul, where Adam is to be honored with a Louis Braille Award. The stagecoach, which also carries a pregnant young woman (Leslie Landon), crashes. Adam's legs are pinned under the wreckage, and Mary, though blind, has to go in search of help for him, the mother-to-be and the injured driver. Mary falls and hits her head, which is actually providential. Landon neatly cuts from a shot of the Oleson wagon to the stagecoach rolling along. After the coach crashes (a stock shot filmed for a 1967 episode of *Gunsmoke* and used by several other series), the camera pulls back from the damaged vehicle to a ground level shot of the unconscious driver. The sun shining on Mary's old eyeglasses starts a fire that brings Charles and Jonathan to the site of the accident. Doc Baker says the mother's ribs are cracked, but the baby is all right, and Adam's legs are only fractured, not broken. Both outcomes are miracles, the third being the signal fire. Mary says she has no idea how it started. Landon cuts away from Baker's office and has the camera move in on Mary's shattered glasses.

Landon's "The Halloween Dream" (10-29-79), a rather inconsequential but entertaining installment, was filmed partly in Arizona and is an intentionally silly cavalry vs. Indians tale. Before attending Nellie Oleson's Halloween party, Albert, who has been reading a book about Indians, dreams that he and Laura are mixed up in frontier hostilities. Amusingly, the guest cast includes Philip Carey and Frank De Kova, who frequently portrayed soldiers and Indians, respectively.

Victor French is billed as a Special Guest Star in Arthur Heinemann's "The Return of Mr. Edwards" (11-05-79), directed by Landon. *Carter Country* was history, and French, despite the hurt feelings caused by his voluntary exit from *Little House* in 1977, welcomed the opportunity to be reunited with his former partner. "I understand why Michael was upset," he said. "It was like I had deserted him. But after I heard there was a problem, I went to talk to him directly and explained everything. It was all settled and forgotten in five minutes." Also returning were Bonnie Bartlett as Grace, and Kyle Richards as Alicia. After learning that Isaiah has been seriously injured by a falling tree and become embittered, Charles and Laura help him regain a sense of purpose and love of life. Landon punctuates a couple of gripping scenes, first by filming Isaiah at ground level as he crawls across the floor, and shooting a close up of Isaiah's hands as he breaks off a stick to trip a rifle trigger in a suicide attempt. Regarding future appearances by French, Landon said, "I haven't decided how often he'll be on. We'll see how the season develops." Viewers would have to wait another two years before seeing Isaiah Edwards again.

In "The King is Dead" (11-12-79), written and directed by Landon, Charles and Jonathan become involved with Milo Stavroupolis, a broken down wrestler once regarded as the best in Europe. Leo Gordon, usually cast as a heavy, plays Milo as a proud and sensitive man who continues to wrestle in order to afford medication for his ill wife, Anna. Jimmy Hart (Ray Walston), Milo's crooked manager, cons Jonathan into beating Milo in a match that has been fixed. Later, to prove he still has what it takes to be a champion, Milo fights a younger wrestler and wins, but the strain is too much, and Milo dies. Landon begins the episode on a close up of Milo's hands as he carries flowers to a vase. Anna's death is revealed in a letter from her in which she says—as a voice-over—"living is a temporary state; loving is forever," followed by a doctor (in another voice-over) saying that Anna had died Thursday morning. Milo hallucinates seeing Anna, telling her he wanted to be a real champ for her again, like in the old days. As they reach for one another, he says, "Love is forever." Jonathan checks his pulse and discovers him dead. The camera pulls back to an overhead shot of Jonathan standing over Milo in a darkened room.

Landon directed Don Balluck's "Crossed Connections" (12-10-79), John T. Dugan's "Whatever Happened to the Class of '56?" (01-14-80), and Vince R. Gutierrez's "Darkness is My Friend" (01-21-80), all varied change of pace episodes (Harriet Oleson wreaks havoc as operator of the town's new telephone system, Charles and Caroline attend a grange convention in Milwaukee, escaped convicts take refuge in the blind school), in workmanlike fashion. The latter is particularly suspenseful, with Landon making considerable use of his signature shadow-and-light effects.

However, there is not much light in evidence during the tragic two-hour Landon epic "May We Make Them Proud" (02-04-80), which was nominated for an Outstanding Cinematography Emmy (Ted Voigtlander) and sets the stage for Merlin Olsen's eventual departure from the series. Alice Garvey and Mary's baby perish when the blind school burns down in a fire accidentally set by Albert and a friend. Jonathan and Andy are shattered by Alice's death; Mary goes into shock; and a guilt ridden Albert runs away in search of his real father. Landon is at the top of his game as both a writer and visual artist, the story consistently engaging and filled with inventive scenes: the camera moves in on a pipe left smoldering in a box of rags; Mary's smiling face is reflected in a mirror inside a music box; Albert steps out of the shadows to listen to Charles and Laura discuss the cause of the fire; the funeral is shot from a distance with gravestones in the foreground; a silent long shot of Walnut Grove's citizens as the wind blows around them. Landon injects necessary levity by having Nellie hit a complaining customer with a raw chicken, followed by an emotional scene of Charles telling a mourning Jonathan that Alice would not him to wallow in grief.

Landon concluded the sixth season by preparing for the seventh with the two-part "He Loves Me, He Loves Me Not" (May 5 and 12, 1980), chronicling the rocky romance of Laura and Almonzo, and introducing the late Steve Tracy as Nellie Oleson's husband, Percival Dalton. Almonzo proposes to Laura, but the couple promise Charles they will not marry for one more year. Percival comes to Walnut Grove to instruct Nellie in how to cook and manage her restaurant, and Caroline goes to work there in order to fund a new blind school in Sleepy Eye. Writer Landon juggles these plot points—and more— and keeps the story moving briskly along by, in part, filming at such varied locations as Simi Valley, Golden Oak Ranch, and the exterior Western set at Warner Bros.

Prior to the start of season seven—three more than he originally thought the series would run—Landon told the press that *Little House* would be "most definitely over at the end of year eight." This was not necessarily due to declining popularity, as the show climbed back into the top ten (for the second and last time), but because of "many contractual agreements" and the fact that Landon was eager to launch other projects. As he had for the previous season, he directed another thirteen episodes, eight of which he also wrote. A ninth script was helmed by the trusted William F. Claxton.

The seventh year began with "Laura Ingalls Wilder" (September 22 and 29), another two-part episode which Landon wrote and directed. The tumultuous courtship of Laura and Almonzo continues with her torn between becoming and teacher or a wife, and him struggling to succeed as a fledgling farmer. Since the viewer suspects everything will eventually work out for them in the end, Landon's challenge was to make the characters' dilemma interesting, and he succeeded without falling into the trap of predictability. Yet the subplot involving Almonzo's sister, Eliza, and her failed pursuit of Harve Miller (James Cromwell), a neighboring farmer, is actually more intriguing. Benefiting mainly from a touching performance by Lucy Lee Flippen, the otherwise joyous conclusion ends on a bittersweet note as Eliza, writing in her journal, lies that she "has never been happier." Landon calls on his legendary sense of humor when dealing with the subject of Nellie Oleson's pregnancy: Over a long shot of Doc Baker's office, Nellie tells her mother she is expecting, followed by the sound of Harriet falling on the floor. Harriet faints again in church after Reverend Alden announces to the congregation that she is going to be a grandmother.

"Fight, Team, Fight!" (10-13-80), written by Don Balluck and directed by Landon, stresses the importance of education, and makes the point that winning is not everything. The prospect of watching two teams of frontier teenagers playing football may not strike one as particularly noteworthy viewing, but Landon manages to capture the action on the field, as well as the drama off of it, with his usual creative eye.

Landon's "The Silent Cry" (10-20-80) is, like "Someone Please Love Me," a rewrite of a *Bonanza* script (1972's "The Sound of Sadness"). Houston (Dub Taylor), the caretaker of the blind school in Sleepy Eye, gives shelter to two boys who run away from the orphanage when a childless couple wants to adopt one, but not the other.

William F. Claxton directed Landon's "Portrait of Love" (10-27-80), largely a story of Caroline's involvement with Annie Crane (Madeline Stowe), a former blind school student who, despite her limitation, has become a gifted painter. Jeremy Unger, an art dealer, arranges for an exhibition of her work in Sleepy Eye. Annie and her adoptive parents are excited until the woman who gave her up for adoption at the age of two wants to make contact. Even though her mother, Marge, is ill, Annie wants nothing to do with her. It is not until the end of the episode that Annie—and the viewer—learn that her birth mother is also blind. Landon continues to use the Oleson family as a source of laughs, having Harriet refuse to allow Percival to sleep with his pregnant wife Nellie.

After directing Don Balluck's largely comedic "Divorce, Walnut Grove Style" (11-10-80), Landon directed his own "Dearest Albert, I'll Miss You" (11-17-80), a lesson in honesty. Albert and Leslie

Barton, his Minneapolis pen pal, lie to each other in their letters. While he exaggerates his accomplishments as a student and athlete, she tells him she is the captain of her basketball team and a dancer, but is really confined to a wheelchair. Albert decides to tell Leslie the truth about himself, joining Charles on a trip to Minneapolis. Not until the end of the episode do the young correspondents learn they are both guilty of deception.

In Landon's two-part "To See the Light" (December 1 and 8), a concussion caused by an explosion restores Adam Kendall's sight. The aftermath leads to a series of dramatic developments which affect his relationship with Mary, due not only to his desire to become a lawyer, but because he can now experience a world she can no longer see. Landon imparts Adam's elation at being able to see by showing him running in slow motion, deliberately splashing across a stream, and raising his arms in victory as the camera pulls back to reveal the beautiful landscape before him. The more serious moments are balanced by doses of Landon humor, from—as usual—the problems of the Olseons (Harriet's weight) to such amusing visuals as the kitchen of Nellie's restaurant being filled with popped corn, and a wagon labeled McCray & Co., a nod to producer Kent McCray. Larry Germain received an Emmy nomination for Outstanding Achievement in Hairstyling for both parts of this episode.

Carole and Michael Raschella's "Come Let Us Reason Together" (01-12-81) concerns a clash of cultures as the Olesons and Percival's Jewish parents disagree about the faith in which Nellie and Percival's children should be raised. When they finally reach a compromise, director Landon ends the scene with a close up of the four grandparents holding hands.

Never one to shy away from controversy if he felt the cause was justified, Landon risked offending *Little House* fans with the two-part "Sylvia" (February 9 and 16), both parts preceded by a warning that the shows could be too disturbing for some viewers. Reaffirming his belief that "family entertainments doesn't have to be sweetness and light," his title character, one of Albert's classmates, is a young girl who has matured early and is raped by a masked stranger. The situation is complicated by her overly strict father, who orders her to keep quiet about the attack and forbids her to spend time with Albert, who says he wants to marry Sylvia when he learns her secret.

Tragedy was not uncommon on *Little House*, but the outcome of "Sylvia" is most likely not what the majority of viewers expected, a credit to Landon's writing skills. The episode also abounds with appropriately cogent shots: extreme close ups of the rapist's leering eye; a dropped bunch of flowers at the moment of the attack; the rapist's mask in the foreground in one of the last scenes. When Sylvia's father says he is selling the farm and moving where no one knows them, he stands in darkness, with Sylvia's face highlighted. An impressive close up of flowers and the water running in Plum Creek begins the sequence of Albert running away to be with Sylvia, leaving behind the Ingalls' whimpering dog, Bandit. Landon effectively concludes the story by reprising an earlier shot of Albert and Sylvia kissing in the woods, a sad reference to what might have been. Ted Voigtlander's camerawork garnered him another Emmy nomination.

Directing Don Balluck's two-part script for "The Lost Ones" (May 4 and 11), Landon laid ground for the eighth and final season of *Little House* with him as star. After their parents are killed in a wagon accident, James Cooper (Jason Bateman) and his sister Cassandra (Missy Francis) are adopted by Charles and Caroline, but not without the customary dramatic tension familiar to faithful followers of the series. (Viewers also saw the last of Jonathan and Andy Garvey, Merlin Olsen destined *Father Murphy*, for a Michael Landon production of his own, later in the year.) Significant visuals include Charles' wagon rolling slowly, the Coopers' graves in the foreground; a silent long shot of Reverend Alden speaking with a farmer interested in adopting the children; Cassandra crying as James is whipped off-camera; the children looking insignificant amid the vast countryside as they attempt to run away. David Rose's music for the first half of this episode resulted in yet another Emmy nomination.

In its last season featuring the Ingalls family, *Little House* slipped to #25 in the 1981-82 ratings, at least some its fan base eroded by *That's Incredible*, a documentary style reality show on ABC that ranked #28 at the end of the season. Except for *Father Murphy*, Landon's latest creation, the residents of Walnut Grove were virtually alone as representatives of family entertainment on a prime time schedule dominated by such situation comedies as *The Jeffersons* and *Three's Company*, and the adult dramas *Dallas*, *Falcon Crest* and their ilk.

Writer/director Landon began the season by introducing Allison Balson as Nancy, the Olesons' adopted daughter, in the two-part "The Reincarnation of Nellie" (October 5 and 12). An even more irritating brat than Nellie, the new character revived some of the flavor of earlier years and allowed Landon to share more of his fatherly wisdom. Adam and Mary (Melissa Sue Anderson now listed among the guest stars) ride off into the sunset (actually New York, where Percival and Nellie are also said to be), giving the Walnut Grove citizens more opportunity to take center stage as the season unfolded. (In a rare oversight, the blacksmith shop is shown as still being owned by Irv Hartwig, the villain of the previous season's "Sylvia.")

Landon directed story editor Chris Abbott's "A Wiser Heart" (11-02-81), largely filmed on location at Old Tucson, wherein Laura travels to Arizona to attend a writing seminar with sister-in-law Eliza (special guest Lucy Lee Flippen), who tells her they can support themselves with part-time teaching jobs. Making her third appearance on the show is Leslie Landon, this time as a restaurant worker.

"Gambini the Great" (11-09-81), written by Jeri Taylor, concerns a visit to Walnut Grove by an aging Houdini-like escape artist whose stunts Albert wants to emulate. Director Landon's customary use of shadows and light is on display in the very first sequence, where Gambini attempts to free himself from a wooden coffin covered with burning hay. One of the final scenes benefits from another of Landon's regular but potent devices, Reverend Alden's voice heard over a long shot of a funeral service held beyond some trees.

John Hawkins and B.W. Sandefur teamed up to write "Chicago" (11-23-81), for which Landon directed the return of Victor French as Isaiah Edwards, last seen in 1979, and billed as a Special Guest Star. Charles and Isaiah go to Chicago to investigate the allegedly accidental death of Isaiah's adopted son, John, who had been working there as a newspaper reporter. A naturally somber tale, Landon once again employs darkness and rain as characters, particularly in the scene where Isaiah, in a gloomy hotel room, stares out a rain-streaked window. Close-ups of hands—a mortician's and Charles'—enhance two crucial moments.

"A Christmas They Never Forgot" (12-21-81), written by Don Balluck and directed by Landon, finds the Ingalls clan—including a visiting Adam and Mary—stranded in their little house by a raging snowstorm, during which they reminisce about past Christmases. Included is a flashback to the *Little House* pilot movie, for which Victor French receives another Special Guest credit. (Curiously, Linwood Boomer is listed with the regular cast at the beginning of the episode, but Melissa Sue Anderson's name appears among the guests in the end credits.)

Carole and Michael Raschella's "No Beast So Fierce" (01-04-82) gave Landon another chance to work with two of his favorite subjects: kids and dogs. A boy ridiculed by his classmates because he stutters bonds with a half-wild dog that distrusts people, aided by the considerable efforts of Charles, Caroline and James. Landon makes the most of L.A.'s Franklin Canyon location, filming mist rising off the lake; a wagon rolling along from the dog's point-of-view, shooting from behind the animal's head; a long shot of the dog running in a sliver of light; the camera tracking slowly down from the top of a pine tree to Caroline emerging from the foliage.

For "The Legacy" (01-25-82), written by Vince R. Gutierrez, director Landon was able to return to the modern world for the first time since *The Loneliest Runner*, specifically Acton, Minnesota, circa 1982. Opening with another of his favored symbols—flowers—he has the camera reveal a pickup truck playing country music, a hand fiddling with the air conditioning dial. The passengers, a married couple, are antique hunters who pull into a barnyard where an auction is taking place. The camera zeroes in on an old table with the initials C.I. carved into it, the weathered wood suddenly appearing fresh as the camera pulls back to reveal Charles Ingalls and Jack Prescott (Claude Earl Jones) carrying the table into a furniture store in Sleepy Eye. The episode is essentially a tale of how the mass production of the Industrial Age encroached on the world of individual craftsmen in 1885, as experienced from Charles' perspective. Although discouraged, he ultimately reminds himself that he has children who will remember him, and that they are his most important legacy. Returning to the present day at the conclusion, Charles' table sells for $125, the young couple wondering if they will ever find out the identity of the craftsman.

With series beginning to slip in the ratings, Landon responded by directing a pair of two-hour episodes—"Days of Sunshine, Days of Sorrow" (February 15 and 22)—the first written by Don Balluck, the second by Chris Abbott. In classic *Little House* fashion, there is tragedy (Almonzo stricken by both diphtheria and a stroke), joy (Laura gives birth to baby Rose), the return of a familiar face (Lucy Lee Flippen as Eliza), catastrophic weather (hailstorm and tornado), symbolism (geraniums), humor, surprises and plot twists—all kept moving briskly and visually interesting by Landon.

In Vince R. Gutierrez's "A Promise to Keep" (03-01-82), directed by Landon, Victor French returns as Isaiah Edwards for the third time. The death of his son, John, has turned him into a hopeless drunk, and Grace has kicked him out of their house. He lies, telling Charles that Grace will be joining him in Walnut Grove for the christening of Laura's daughter, when in reality she plans to divorce him. Isaiah manages to keep his drinking problem a secret until his misjudgment results in Albert almost losing a leg, and Charles telling him he does not want to ever see him again. Landon emphasizes the lasting bond between Isaiah and Laura with a close up of their hands clasping as Laura helps her lifelong friend into a wagon. When Reverend Alden baptizes Rose beside Plum Creek, the camera begins with a long shot of the ceremony, dropping to pan across the line of family members in a medium close shot. Laura hands Rose to Isaiah, the camera following the baby, then freezing on Isaiah's smiling profile.

The eighth season ended with the two-part episode "He Was Only Twelve" (May 3 and 10), directed by Landon, who also wrote the second half. Curiously, the first is credited to Paul W. Cooper despite it being nearly a scene-by-scene rewrite of Landon's *Bonanza* script "He Was Only Seven." After James is seriously wounded by bank robbers, Charles, Isaiah and Albert track down the perpetrators. Part two, which received Emmy nominations for composer David Rose and cinematographer Ted Voigtlander, opens with a voice-over by Laura saying that James survived an operation but remained in a coma as the camera zooms in on the Little House. Doc Baker's examination of James begins on a close up of the boy's eye, switching to a shot of the doctor wearing a headband equipped with a light and mirror. When Baker tells Charles a miracle is needed, Charles replies, "Go away, Hiram"—a rare utterance of Baker's first name. Charles is convinced he can bring about a miracle himself, building a tall stone altar topped by a cross. His and James's journey to the site of the altar is depicted by a montage of horses walking, wagon wheels spinning, James in the back of the wagon, and Charles holding the reins. Landon shows the passage of time by having Charles grow a beard while he and James wait for a miracle to occur. The appearance of a guardian angel in the guise of an old man is, perhaps, a preview of what would be Landon's next starring vehicle. As for *Little House on the Prairie*, the saga of the family Ingalls ends with this strange story of faith, the final scene a wide shot of Charles, James, Caroline and Isaiah in the lush setting of Golden Oak Ranch.

PHOTO GALLERY

Rex Ingram and Landon in *God's Little Acre*, **1958**

The Cartwrights: Dan Blocker, Lorne Greene, Pernell Roberts, Landon, 1960

Lorne Greene and David Canary in "To Die in Darkness," Landon's directorial debut as a director on *Bonanza* (May 5, 1968)

Johnny Whitaker, Michele Tobin, Dan Blocker in "A Dream to Dream" (*Bonanza* April 14, 1968), written by Landon

George Spell and Dan Blocker in "The Wish" (March 9, 1969), Landon's favorite episode of those he wrote and directed for *Bonanza*

David Canary with the Cartwrights at Incline Village for Landon's "Kingdom of Fear," filmed in 1967 but not aired until 1971

Landon with Bonnie Bedelia in "Forever" (September 12, 1972), the epic two-hour *Bonanza* written and directed by Landon

Landon directing Jack Albertson in Bonanza's "The Sound of Sadness" (December 5, 1972), also written by Landon

The Men of Walnut Grove—Richard Bull, Michael Landon, Dean Butler, Dabbs Greer, 1981

Victor French and Landon in *Highway to Heaven*

Lorne Greene with Landon, his longtime "son", last worked together on *Highway to Heaven* in 1985, two years before Greene's death

Chapter 5
Father Murphy
(1981–1983)

Moses Gunn, Katherine Cannon and Merlin Olsen, 1981

"There's a tendency to think that, because you're paid to act, you've got to *do* something. When you're Merlin's size, mere physical presence is enough."

Michael Landon, 1981

Impressed by his portrayal of Jonathan Garvey in *Little House on the Prairie*, NBC asked Merlin Olsen if he would be interested in headlining a series of his own. While he was open to the idea, Olsen told the network he wanted to wait until he had more experience—and only if Michael Landon was involved in the project. Consequently, 1981 found Landon simultaneously launching the eighth season of *Little House* and the first of *Father Murphy*, which he also created and executive produced. Olsen starred as the title character, John Michael Murphy, an 1870s frontiersman who travels to Dakota Territory with his dog, Mine (also the name of the puppy in Landon's "Remember Me"), to prospect for gold, and ends up masquerading as a priest to save a school full of orphans from being confined to a dismal workhouse.

Joining the regular cast of *Father Murphy* as Moses Gage was Moses Gunn, who had played Joe Kagan in numerous episodes of *Little House*. Romantic interest was provided by Katherine Cannon as Mae Woodward, the local schoolteacher. Of the two dozen or so children under Murphy's wing, the most prominent were Timothy Gibbs as Will Adams, Lisa Trusel as Lizette Winkler, and Scott Mellini as Ephraim Winkler. In addition to the usual roundup of rough Western antagonists were Charles Tyner as Howard Rodman and Ivy Bethune as Miss Tuttle, the dreaded Claymore Workhouse administrators.

The two-hour pilot, written and directed by Landon, debuted on Tuesday, November 3, scheduled against the enormously popular situation comedies *Happy Days* and *Laverne & Shirley* on ABC. This formidable competition was to prevent the eventual thirty-three episodes of *Father Murphy*—eight of which involved Landon's participation as writer and/or director—from attracting the audience it deserved. Fortunately for admirers of Landon's productions, the series was issued on DVD in two separate volumes in 2004.

In the premiere episode, filmed partly at Old Tucson, Murphy gets a job as a freight driver for crooked town boss Paul Garrett, but is promptly fired for exposing the crooked roulette wheel in Garrett's saloon. Partnering with prospector Moses Gage and orphan Will Adams, Murphy decides to try his luck panning for gold. When Garrett's henchmen blow up the mining camp in order to buy up the prospectors' claims, the local priest is killed, and Howard Rodman and Miss Tuttle from the nearby workhouse swoop in to take the newly orphaned children. Schoolteacher Mae Woodward pleads with them to wait until another priest can bring assistance from the church, but they turn her down. In the end, Mae and the children move into the saloon of an abandoned mining camp called Gold Hill, which makes no difference to Rodman and Tuttle until Murphy shows up in the dead priest's robe and tells them he is taking over.

Murphy's deception is revealed to a real, younger priest in the first regular episode, "Eggs, Milk and a Dry Bed" (11-10-81), also written and directed by Landon, and which includes a subplot regarding the issue of bedwetting. The new priest insists he is equally as capable as Murphy in taking care of the Gold Hill children, but soon learns otherwise. Landon, who by now had directing down to a personalized science, concludes the episode by having the camera pull back from a window of the orphanage to show the children eating inside.

"By the Bear That Bit Me," a two-part episode (December 1 and 8) directed by William F. Claxton, was co-written by Ron Bishop (a frequent contributor to *Gunsmoke*), Steve Hayes and Landon, and features a standout performance by the late, great Jack Elam as a dying mountain man. Playing his youthful companion is Shannen Doherty, soon to become a member of the *Little House* ensemble.

Landon wrote "The Spy" (02-16-82), again directed by Claxton. When Archibald, the son of workhouse head Rodman is expelled from school, his grandmother (amusingly played by Charles Tyner in drag) suggests sending the boy to Gold Hill. Rodman believes Archibald can assist his attempts to close the school by acting as a spy. A scene where Archibald injures a dove by hitting it with a rock was likely inspired by an event from Landon's life. In an interview with writer Tom Ito, he said, "I can remember walking home from school with a bunch of kids, and you know how there'll be a whole bunch of birds on a lawn? And how you want to scare the birds away? I picked up a rock and threw the rock, hit the bird on the head, and killed it! It was one of so many birds. I felt awful!" In the episode, the dove is nursed back to health, as are its hatchlings. (*Bonanza* fans will recognize music used from as far back as 1963's "Hoss and the Leprechauns.")

In "The Heir Apparent" (02-23-82), another Landon/Claxton collaboration, Rachel Hansen, a wealthy widow wants to adopt Will, who has come to consider Murphy a father figure, and send him to New York for a first rate education. In a story more about love than education (both favorite Landon themes), Murphy asks Rachel, "You will love him, won't you, ma'am?" much the same as Charles Ingalls questioned Harriet Oleson's rich cousin who wanted to adopt Alicia in "Remember Me." Will ends up staying at Gold Hill, Murphy saying he loves him, which is why he wanted him to have education and security. Will promises to keep on learning.

"The Dream Day" (03-14-82), a Landon script directed by Maury Dexter, returns to another of Landon's familiar subjects: the potential separation of siblings. The Gold Hill orphanage sponsors an open house for couples interested in adopting a child, causing trauma for two brothers. A prospective parent is played appealingly by Leslie Landon, her fourth appearance in one of her father's productions.

Producing the only season of *Little House: A New Beginning* and attempting to spend more time with his family, Landon's creative involvement with the second season of *Father Murphy* was limited to reworking his "Bonanza" script "Dead Wrong" as "John Michael Murphy, R.I.P.," directed by Joseph Pevney. The main asset of the episode, in which Murphy and Gage are mistaken for outlaws in the town of Sunville, is the guest cast of colorful character actors, including Eddie Quillan (one of Landon's favorites) and Parley Baer.

NBC reran the first season of *Father Murphy* on Sunday evenings from March to July of 1982 before moving it back to Tuesday, when the second season began in September. In December, after only eleven episodes, the series was pulled from the schedule. Two unaired episodes were burned off in June and September of 1983, by which time *Father Murphy* had been canceled for good. To fill a programming gap, the network reran episodes on Sunday during the spring of 1984.

Landon accepted most of the responsibility for the fate of *Father Murphy*. "It was the first time I tried to be involved in more than one show, and I'm not a good delegator of authority. It just isn't one of my strong points. I had a show doing well and network called up and said, 'We'd love for you to do another show, any kind of show you want.' That's a great carrot. It makes your ego feel real good. You think, 'I should be able to do that, other people have tons of shows on the air.' Well, I learned it wasn't for me. I'm happy just doing one show at a time."

Chapter 6
The Little House: Part Two
Love Is Forever
Sam's Son
(1982–1984)

Landon directing *Little House* at Paramount Studios, 1978

"I got a lot of the scenes from *Little House* from my own kids. I think the older you get and the more children you have, the more you realize how quickly that child is going to grow up. You tend to want to spend even more time than you spent in the beginning. I mean I don't want to work weekends anymore and miss all that."

Michael Landon, 1983

In early April 1982, Landon announced that neither he nor Karen Grassle would be returning to *Little House on the Prairie*, appended for its ninth season as *A New Beginning*. "I just felt it was time to step aside and let some of the younger characters on the show take over," he said. "Much of our audience consists of children, and I think they identify with youngsters on the program." Continuing as executive producer, he also wrote seven scripts, directed three episodes and appeared in two.

Now headlining the cast were Melissa Gilbert, Victor French, Richard Bull and Katherine MacGregor. Among the new additions was Leslie Landon, in the role of schoolteacher Etta Plum. "You know," said her father, "when I was writing the new schoolteacher part for *Little House*, Leslie immediately came to mind, but I rejected the thought. But then it occurred to me: Don't we worry so much in this business about being accused of nepotism that we end up not giving our own kids the same breaks as strangers? If I were a lawyer, a car dealer, I'd want my kid to join the firm. Why should show business be any different?" Leslie had already been given small parts in three episodes, as well as another on *Father Murphy*, and Landon judged his daughter's talent as "absolutely great."

Little House: A New Beginning premiered on September 27—eight days after Landon was honored with the Founder's Award at that year's Emmy ceremony—in the familiar Monday night time slot occupied by the original version. Landon's two-part "Times Are Changing," directed by Maury Dexter, introduced Stan Ivar and Pamela Roylance as John and Sarah Carter, the new owners of the Ingalls homestead. Their sons, Jeb and Jason, were portrayed by Lindsay Kennedy and David Friedman. Landon makes a brief cameo as Charles, who goes inside the house for a final look at the pump he installed in the kitchen, and the fireplace mantel with his and Caroline's initials carved into the wood. Laura joins him to reminisce, their tearful embrace interrupted when Jeb and Jason burst on the scene. Sarah, noticing Charles' tears, asks John to promise they will never move. Charles becomes emotional once more when Almonzo, Doc Baker, Isaiah Edwards, Nels Oleson and Reverend Alden present him with a new suit to wear as a clothing salesman in Iowa. Jenny (Shannen Doherty), the young daughter of Royal Wilder, Almonzo's brother, moves in with Laura and Almonzo after her father succumbs to a heart attack. Blaming herself for Royal's death, Jenny goes into an emotional tailspin and attempts suicide by drowning but is rescued by Jeb. Observing tradition, humorous moments are supplied by Harriet Oleson, who is determined to contribute to Sarah Carter's newspaper. In one scene, Isaiah remarks that Harriet would make a train take a dirt road.

"Little Lou" (10-25-82), directed by Victor French, found Landon adapting an old *Bonanza* script to fit *Little House*, in this case 1970's "It's A Small World." Billy Barty is particularly good as Lou Bates, a little person, who runs afoul of the prejudiced Harriet Oleson. When Nancy falls down an old well, Lou is the only person small enough to rescue her, forcing Harriet to apologize for her short temper. Lou, accepting her apology, jokes that if anyone has a short temper it is him, but adds that he is not a small man.

Combining his use of flowers as symbols of life, and his affection for older people, Landon wrote "Marvin's Garden" (01-03-83), one of his finest stories for the last season of the series. Directed by Michael Rhodes, the episode features special guest star Ralph Bellamy as Marvin Haynes, a semi-retired physician whose eyesight is failing. He helps Jenny recover from a partial stroke, and also assists her in nursing an injured bird. After Marvin can no longer see the flowers he loves, Jenny identifies the ones she picks for him on their walks together.

Another of Landon's *Bonanza* episodes, "The Younger Brothers' Younger Brother" from 1972, was rewritten as "The Older Brothers" (01-17-83), with Victor French directing himself in a tale of Isaiah being mistaken for an outlaw.

Landon returned to the show as Charles for the two-hour "Home Again," (02-07-83), which he also wrote and directed. The episode begins with a shot of a pair of hands taking a hat from a store's display window and being carried to a customer. The hands belong to none other than Charles Ingalls, his hair now white, working as a clerk for Janes & Son. (The senior Janes is portrayed by Charles Tyner, the odious Howard Rodman from *Father Murphy*.) A policeman tells Charles that Albert has been caught stealing again, prompting Charles to take his rebellious son from the negative influences of the big city and back to the simplicity of Walnut Grove. When their stagecoach passes by the former Ingalls farm,

Charles remarks that the place is looking good. Albert is not impressed. What Charles does not know is that Albert has developed a drug habit, which contrasts with a subplot concerning Jason Carter's desire for a pair of glasses he does not really need. Unlike the similarly dark and atypical "Sylvia," this episode has an upbeat conclusion, Albert confessing his addiction to Miss Plum's students as the camera scans their young faces. "I created family relationships where people stay together because they communicate," Landon said two years later. "Even *Little House* had problems even though people thought it was soft and sentimental family fantasy. In the show I had a son on drugs and we showed it as realistically as it's ever been shown on TV. We showed him going through withdrawal cold turkey. No one's ever done that before. I think that got through to a lot of kids."

"For the Love of Blanche" (03-07-83), an amusing installment written and directed by Landon, deals with Isaiah's "adoption" of an orangutan named Blanche, formerly owned by a man claiming to be Buffalo Bill. The ape wreaks predictable havoc in Walnut Grove, and Harriet Oleson insists that Blanche be killed. Isaiah pretends to execute Blanche, which is captured in an effective long shot. When Isaiah has to say farewell to Blanche, Landon manages to wring pathos out of even a largely comic episode. The final shot, freezing on Blanche, is accompanied by Isaiah's voice referring to her as "a very special person."

Landon directed Don Balluck's "Hello and Goodbye" (03-21-83), which turned out to be the final episode of both the season and the series. NBC had initially renewed the show for thirteen episodes, and then ordered an additional eight, but ratings continued to decline as those for the opposing *That's Incredible* on ABC rose. Although one of only four programs the network had in the top thirty, *Little House: A New Beginning* (tied with *Happy Days* at #28) was canceled. Melissa Gilbert and Victor French protested publicly, but to no avail. The sole consolation was NBC's agreement to allow Landon to officially end the series with a trio of made-for-television movies. "Hello and Goodbye," which was to have been a setup for a tenth season, instead served as a prelude to the last days of Walnut Grove. Robert Casper joins the cast as the eccentric Sherwood Montague, and Isaiah decides to move into Laura's boarding house after losing custody of a mute boy he has been caring for. In the last shot of the series, Landon has the camera pull back from light shining in a round window of the boarding house.

"Love is Forever" (04-03-83)

In 1978 director Hall Bartlett purchased the rights to the true story of Australian journalist John Everingham's incredible rescue of his Laotian fiancée, Keo Sirisomphone. Braving a hail of bullets fired by Communist secret police, the couple swam across the bottom of the Mekong River to freedom in Thailand, a daring feat Bartlett was certain would translate beautifully to the screen. After writing the script himself, he set up a series of production deals which, in typical Hollywood fashion, collapsed. In early 1982, 20th Century-Fox committed to the project. Landon, who had not appeared in a feature film since 1959, was signed to star after being recommended by Bartlett's daughters, both of them *Little House* fans. The seven-million-dollar budget included nearly five million that Landon convinced NBC to invest in exchange for U.S. broadcast rights. (When released theatrically in Canada and foreign markets a few months before the network airing, the film's title was *Comeback*.) Although the bulk of filming took place on location in Thailand, underwater sequences were shot in Crystal River, Florida, where the water was clearer and less treacherous than the Mekong.

Skilled in virtually every aspect of filmmaking, and accustomed to working with a crew that operated like the proverbial well-oiled machine, Landon grew impatient and was understandably frustrated by the slower pace of a feature production, entitled *Love is Forever* when televised in April. He also felt a responsibility to see that the end result was successful, considering his longtime employer, NBC, had a substantial financial interest in the project. Fox executives were pleased with the finished film and declared Landon's performance the finest of his career. Unfortunately, alleged behind-the-scenes squabbling between Bartlett and Landon were blown out of proportion by the tabloids, overshadowing a basically solid and suspenseful real life adventure.

As Everingham, the last western journalist remaining in Indochina, circa April 1978, Landon delivers an impassioned speech on the plight of the Laotians to Keo (Moira Chen), engages in a kickboxing match with a vile Russian general (Jurgen Prochnow), and is arrested, roughed up and chained. Having watched him in 19th century costumes for more than two decades, it is something of a novelty to see Landon in contemporary garb (including scuba gear), and puffing on cigarettes for the first time since the 1959 *Zane Grey* episode "Living is a Lonesome Thing."

In an interview shortly after wrapping *Love is Forever*, Landon said, "I discovered a long time ago that it's a lot easier to do the work than to argue with somebody else about it. If I had to pick the one job that I like all of the time, I'd have to say directing. There's never a day I don't like that. I really enjoy it. Writing—some days you're cooking and some days you're not. It gets a little scary sometimes."

Little House: "The Last Farewell" (02-06-84)

The cast of *Little House*, including Landon, reunited for the telefilm "Look Back to Yesterday" (12-12-83), which found Walnut Grove in the midst of yet another recession, and Albert Ingalls doomed by a fatal blood disease. Less than two months later, a press report revealed, "The *Little House on the Prairie* will be the only thing left when Ma and Pa Ingalls' fictional town of Walnut Grove will be dynamited to oblivion in a special two-hour episode of the long-running television show." The Simi Valley property was owned by Newhall Land and Development, which wanted the land restored to its natural state when the series ended. That was more than fine with Landon, who did not want to later see another company making a commercial or cheap horror film at the site. (Sharp-eyed viewers would recognize the site in the 2006-07 CBS drama *Jericho*.) Spared from demolition were the church/schoolhouse and the Ingalls homestead, although the latter was destroyed in a 2003 wildfire.

Written and directed by Landon, "The Last Farewell," which could have easily been long on sentiment and little else, is instead an absorbing and, yes, sad coda to a classic series. Charles and Caroline (Landon and Grassle billed as special guest stars) return to Walnut Grove for a vacation at the same time as Nathan Lassiter (James Karen), a land developer intent on acquiring the town for its iron ore deposits. Lassiter informs the citizens that their land is not homesteading property as originally thought after a treaty with the Sioux Indians collapsed. Anyone working in Walnut Grove, he adds, will be a salaried employee of Lassiter and Company. Nels threatens legal action, but an attorney tells him and Charles that nothing can be done, even if Lassiter is morally wrong. The townsfolk resolve to defy the court's ruling and stand their ground. When his gang of bullies fails to evict anyone, Lassiter brings in the army, led by a Colonel Forbes. Forbes tells the men of Walnut Grove that he understands their feelings, but has a job to do. Reverend Alden pleads with him to allow the citizens to remain until Easter Sunday, and Forbes agrees, ignoring Lassiter's request to have the town cleared immediately. Later, Laura suggests demolishing the town. Isaiah says that Lassiter might be able to kill Walnut Grove, but its people will be the ones to bury it. Using John Carter's dynamite, Almanzo tearfully blows up his and Laura's boarding house, the debris falling in slow motion. Isaiah, Nels, Doc Baker and Willie Oleson take turns detonating the charges that bring down Hanson's mill, Oleson's Mercantile, Baker's office, and Nellie's restaurant/hotel. The church is damaged, but still stands. Lassiter insists that Forbes arrest everyone, but the officer says no law has been broken. Rather than being able to use his takeover of Walnut Grove as a display of his power to other communities, Lassiter is told that the mayors of nearby towns are planning demolitions of their own. Hearing this, Reverend Alden declares that Walnut Grove did not die in vain. The town was theirs, says Isaiah. Only the land is Lassiter's. The citizens march away from the ruins singing "Onward, Christian Soldiers."

Obeying one of the cardinal rules of screenwriting, Landon finds opportunities for moments of levity during what is a decidedly downbeat story. Before leaving for Walnut Grove, Charles is punched by an irate customer at the hotel he is managing, and has to put a raw steak on his black eye. After Charles plays a tune on his fiddle, Sherwood Montague shows him up by performing "Flight of the Bumblebee" perfectly. Nels will not allow Nancy to have one of the rabbits Jason Carter is raising because her last one died due to lack of care the year before. These humorous moments are woven into a skillful tapestry that includes the expected degree of poignancy. There is a reference to the tree Charles fell out of in the first season of the series, Charles and Caroline are able to spend time in their former homestead, and Reverend Alden stops to gaze at the sign proclaiming Walnut Grove's founding by Lars Hanson in 1840. (Fittingly, there is a final shot of the sign after the closing credits have rolled.)

Director Landon's final *Little House* landmark contains a number of inventive touches: Caroline is reflected in Laura's mirror when they are reunited; the camera slowly pans across the faces of Isaiah, Jenny, Rachel and Willie Oleson, Almonzo and Sherwood as Charles plays his fiddle; concern over the impending fate of Walnut Grove is illustrated by a close up of Reverend Alden's worried countenance; trouble to come is indicated by a close shot of Almonzo's hand grabbing rifle shells; Charles and Caroline clasp hands across the table in their old home. One image in particular—the tearful faces of Isaiah and Jason—shows the effect of the town's imminent fate on Walnut Grove's past and its future. After the buildings have been destroyed, a long shot of Reverend Alden walking among the ruins switches to an effective medium tracking shot. As wagons roll past the Ingalls farm at the conclusion of the episode, the camera moves in on Jason's rabbits, now free, cavorting in the yard. Just as Lassiter is not able to profit from the town of Walnut Grove, neither is Jason successful in profiting from the sale of his rabbits. Yet whereas Lassiter is left with property strewn with rubble, Jason leaves behind life that he has nurtured and will continue near Plum Creek, long after the people who shared the land are gone. No doubt Landon's own feelings were spoken by Sarah Carter (Pamela Roylance): "I'm going to miss this little house."

NOTE: A third *Little House* telefilm, "Bless All the Dear Children," aired out of chronological order on December 17, somewhat anticlimactically. While he was executive producer, Landon did not write, direct or appear in it.

"Sam's Son"
(08-17-84)

In 1984, the Hollywood Chamber of Commerce honored Michael Landon with a star on the Hollywood Walk of Fame, and the Motion Picture and Television Fund Foundation gave him a Golden Boot Award "for significant contribution to the Western genre." Landon, in addition to memorably closing down his Little House, continued to share his multiple talents with the public in another major primetime drama.

First, however, as writer and director he mined his own past for *Sam's Son*, which in some measure can be regarded as a sequel to 1976's *The Loneliest Runner*. The semi-autobiographical film, a Kevin O'Sullivan Production, was released in August 1984 for a limited theatrical run before airing on NBC as a Movie of the Week. The title is, of course, a play on the name Samson, the source of young Landon's belief that his long hair was at least partly responsible for his skill with the javelin. In the opening sequence, Landon, as actor Eugene Orman (nee Orowitz) emerges from a private jet for a movie premiere in his hometown of Colendale (rather than Collingswood) and has the waiting limousine stop by his boyhood home. As he looks at the house, he mutters, "We did it, Sam. The dreamers did it." Flashing back to the 1950s, the Four Aces' rendition of Johnny Mercer's "Dream" appropriately expresses the overall theme of the film. (Other period music used on the soundtrack includes "How High the Moon" by Les Paul and Mary Ford, "Mister Sandman" by the Chordettes, and "Pretend" by Nat "King" Cole.) Gene (Timothy Patrick Murphy) informs his father outright that he wants to be in the movies. Sam Orowitz (Eli Wallach), like Eli Orowitz, wanted to be a writer but makes his living managing a movie theater. Gene's mother, Harriet (Anne Jackson), wants Sam to darken his hair in order to look younger and increase his chances of getting a raise from his employer. When a coach introduces Gene's gym class to the javelin, Gene excels, but the satisfaction he feels is overshadowed by the shame of backing down from a bully who calls him "Jew boy" in front of his girlfriend, Bonnie (Joanna Lee). Not helping matters is the fact that the bully, Bob Woods (Alan Hayes) has designs on Bonnie. Gene tells his father how he chickened out when challenged to a fight, to which Sam replies, "Everyone has a Bob Woods in his life." Gene says he is going to make Sam proud someday, and that he is not just a dreamer. After Bonnie takes up with Bob, Gene concentrates on his ability with the javelin, which the coach tells him is nearly in "scholarship territory." His mother tells him not to get his hopes up—and to get a haircut. But Gene has no intention of losing any of his locks, especially after watching *Samson and Delilah* and hearing Hedy Lamarr tell Victor Mature his power comes from the length of his hair. The school principal, Mr. Collin (none other than James Karen, the villainous Lassiter in "The Last Farewell"), tells Gene he cannot compete athletically unless he gets a haircut. His mother continues to badger him, but Sam sympathizes with his dilemma, having Gene's uncle, a doctor, cover the young man's head with a cast. Sam tells Harriet that a car knocked Gene down, but the injury is not serious—no concussion, just a few stitches. Gene acquires a new girlfriend, Cathy (Hallie Todd), continues to improve with the javelin, knocks Bob Wood out with one punch (shown in slow motion), and snubs Bonnie when she attempts to get back in his good graces. As Gene's future prospects begin to brighten, Sam is not as fortunate. He takes another stab at writing, but receives no encouragement from his wife, who tells him he is only dreaming again. Asking the theater owner (Sam's version of Gene's Bob Wood) for time off to watch Gene audition for a coach from USC is an uncomfortable confrontation, and on the way to the track meet Sam is delayed when forced to retrieve film from a broken down delivery truck. On his second trip carrying the film canisters upstairs to the projection room, he suffers a heart attack. A policeman informs Gene that Sam is in the hospital. Gene, in tears, removes the bandages from his head and throws the javelin—in slow motion—for his father, setting a new record of over 220 feet. At the hospital, a doctor tells Gene that Sam needs a new heart. When Sam dies, the camera moves in on a flashing red light in the room which becomes a flashing red light on the car phone in actor Gene Ormon's limousine. Cathy and his mother are waiting at the Rialto Theater, where the marquee reads: "In Person: Gene Orman." After Gene berates the theater manager—Sam's old boss—for having lights out on the marquee (as the boss did years ago to Sam), the camera pulls back to reveal: "Sam's Son. Written by Sam Orowitz."

As in virtually all of Landon's projects, love and understanding play major role in *Sam's Son*, which can be rightfully considered a tribute to Eli Orowitz. The scenes between Timothy Patrick Murphy and Eli Wallach form the emotional core of the film. At one point, father and son admit they love each other. When Gene tells Sam he is excited to be going to college in California, where all the movies are made, his father apologizes for letting him down, not being able to afford sending him to USC without a scholarship. He says he also let Harriet down, that he was supposed to be a famous writer. Do not make the same mistake he did, Sam warns his son. Do not make promises—people end up feeling too guilty to say "I love you" when the promises go unfulfilled. Later, in the hospital, Sam apologizes for not making it to the meet: "See what I mean about promises? I promised I'd be there." To atone, he reveals that he has written a script called "Sam's Son," telling Gene, "Maybe one day, when you're famous, you could use it." Gene promises he will, to which Sam responds, predictably, "Don't make promises." Just as Landon triumphed over so many obstacles and setbacks in life, so too does Gene Orman, ultimately fulfilling that final promise to Sam.

Sam's Son fared better when televised than it did as a theatrical release, but Landon was philosophical about its fate. "I think an audience tends not to want to pay for something they get for nothing," he said. "I'm a television name, and a very important name in television. And in order to be an important name in features at this point in my life I'd have to be thirty years younger, and I'm not. I'm a fifty-year-old man who is not going to become a superstar at this point in his life in films."

Chapter 7
THE HIGHWAY
(1984–1989)

Landon and Victor French

"I had a hard time selling this one, but I was lucky. I was in a position to get this show on the air. The network was shocked by the good test results."
                                    Michael Landon, 1984

In early 1984 Michael Landon was contemplating leaving NBC, his professional home since 1959. The problem, he told the press, was a breakdown in communication. "I'm not talking about money," he said. "I'm talking about them just coming through with what they said they would do." The previous year, frustrated by the seemingly perpetual turnover of network executives, he remarked, "I've been there longer than anyone else. I've gone through more NBC presidents than you can imagine. I always have to meet these new people and some of those new people don't like the deal you've made with the old people. It's very annoying, to be honest with you. I'm no different than anybody else. I kind of like having a boss, though NBC is not my boss, per se. I want somebody, every once in a while, to say, 'Hey, you did a nice job for us.'"

It was amid this climate that Landon boldly proposed his next project, one that would find him stepping out of the nineteenth century, where viewers were most accustomed to seeing him—and into the contemporary role of Jonathan Smith, an earthbound angel attempting to earn his wings by helping people in need. Predictably, most of the network's top brass balked. Fortunately, Landon had an ally in Brandon Tartikoff, NBC's entertainment president in charge of programming. "I like him a lot," Tartikoff said of Landon. "My dream network would be 22 hours of talent like his." Considering that NBC had finished in third place behind ABC and CBS for the 1983-84 season, with only six programs among the top thirty, the network needed a star with Landon's drawing power. Tartikoff suggested the title *Highway to Heaven*, and a pilot was ordered. If the telefilm became a series, Landon, in addition to acting, writing, directing and producing, would also own the show.

Cast as Jonathan's mortal assistant, an ex-policeman named Mark Gordon, was Landon's former *Little House* co-star, Victor French. Some network executives, already skeptical about the pilot's chances, wanted a younger actor for the part, but Landon refused. "I somehow knew Michael would have enough clout to get it on the air," French said the following year. "We knew there was an audience that wanted to see something besides flying cars and machine guns."

The pilot film tested far beyond the network's expectations, just as the pilot for *Little House on the Prairie* had ten years before. In fact, *Highway to Heaven* was the most enthusiastically received pilot in NBC's history to date, due in part to the performance by John Bleifer (who played the title role in the memorable *Little House* episode "The Craftsman") as an elderly Jewish man. "When I told him how he had tested," said Landon, "that he had tested through the roof, he was a young man of 30 again."

"The critics are going to have a field day with this," Tartikoff predicted after screening the pilot, and he was correct. Most reviews of the September 19 premiere, written and directed by Landon, dismissed *Highway* as more saccharine sentimentality. "I don't much care what they say," Landon responded. "There are an awful lot of people out there who are trying to make people laugh; there are very few shows that can, on a regular basis, give the audience a good cry. I know I can do that—and if I do that well, they [the audience] will be back." At least one critic, John J. O'Connor of the *New York Times*, conceded, "Actually, Mr. Landon seems to have accurately sensed the prevailing mood of the country."

The concept of angels existing among everyday folk is not a new Hollywood tradition, the most prominent examples being *Here Comes Mr. Jordan* (1941), *The Horn Blows at Midnight* (1945), *The Bishop's Wife* (1947), *Heaven Can Wait* (1978) and especially director Frank Capra's *It's A Wonderful Life* (1946), said to be Tartikoff's favorite film. The idea for *Highway to Heaven*—a combination of Capra's classic and the *Route 66* television series—came to Landon while stuck in a Beverly Hills traffic jam. "People were honking at each other," he said. "There is no worse place for that than Beverly Hills; I think that when people have a little bit more money, they really believe that the Red Sea will part and their car *will* go forward. And I thought, 'Why is everybody so angry? If they would just spend that time being nice…It's obvious the flow of traffic is going to go much better if everybody has his opportunity.'"

Following Landon into the production of his third series were many of his loyal crew members, including, among others, producer Kent McCray, casting director Susan McCray, composer David Rose, and cinematographers Ted Voigtlander and Brianne Murphy. Everyone on Team Landon was familiar with their leader's ability to work quickly, efficiently, and conclude each day's shooting in time for them to have dinner with their families. More often than not, episodes were produced under budget, and Landon shared the savings with his employees. Thanks to the professionalism of his crew, Landon was able to take on the Herculean task of appearing in all 111 episodes, writing 22 and directing an astonishing 93, which included all 37 episodes of the fourth and fifth seasons. Only sixteen did not involve his writing or direction.

Essentially an anthology series, *Highway to Heaven* featured a wide variety of characters in an ever-changing number of locales. "I wanted to do a show where people move around," Landon said. "I spent 14 years on the ranch on *Bonanza* and nine years on *Little House on the Prairie*. There are only so many ways you can film a house. People tend to lose their juices if they can't move around and be challenged…So having an angel works out fine. He doesn't have to worry about a job and he's always free to travel."

Anyone expecting the series to be a sermon-of-the-week had no need to worry. "I play down the religious side of the show," Landon said, "even though I don't play down the serious side to it. But the God I believe in is not so egotistical about what you believe in—he'd be more concerned with the sort of human being you are. I have a strong faith in God, and that gives me great security and helps me. I feel obligated in many ways to try to do good things with my work because it's my one means of reaching people."

Landon's primarily goal was to depict society—warts and all—in a positive light, or, in strictly Romantic terms, life as it could and should be, and would be if only people were more respectful to one another. To that end, *Highway to Heaven* tackled such diverse subjects as bigotry, homelessness, pollution, political corruption, substance abuse, and people who are somehow "different", the handicapped in particular. According to Landon, "Stories about individuals coping with their disabilities make the rest of us realize how insignificant our problems really are. These kinds of stories sort of put life into perspective. In turn, handicapped people are pleased to see such stories take their lives out of the closet, allowing the public to see how these challenges have been met and overcome. Most handicapped people want those who are not impaired to look beyond their disabilities and see the person there." While often downbeat—yet usually uplifting—the series did not neglect the element of humor, most frequently in banter exchanged by Jonathan and Mark, as well as in the episodes produced for Halloween, coincidentally Landon's birthday.

Highway to Heaven was an immediate hit on Wednesday evening, trouncing both ABC's popular *The Fall Guy* and the CBS sitcoms *Charles in Charge* and *Dreams* in the weekly ratings and placing #19 in the year-end rankings. Of the first 25 episodes, Landon wrote and directed five, wrote an additional three, and directed thirteen stories contributed by other writers. By now he had directing down to the proverbial science, his distinctive visual style transferring smoothly to modern day settings without becoming clichéd. However, perhaps aware that suburban houses, office buildings, city streets, hospitals and convenience stores are not as enthralling to watch as the towns and prairies of a bygone era, Landon's writing became, by necessity, the most important component of *Highway to Heaven*. In retrospect, the show's emphasis on sharing and caring was a welcome antidote to the alienation and ennui brought on by a society that had become increasingly cynical and self-absorbed. "I thought it would be good to do a show where people could see how much better and healthier it is to go through life using their energy being nice to somebody instead of using it for anger that has no meaning," Landon said. "There's no sense to it. So I came up with the premise for this show."

The two-hour premiere again includes two of the primary objects of Landon's affection, the elderly and dogs, as Jonathan hires on as a handyman and gardener for Havencrest, a retirement home where he gives a reclusive woman named Estelle Wicks ("special guest star" Helen Hayes) a puppy to look after. Also working there is Leslie Gordon, a nurse whose brother, Mark, was a policeman in Oakland for fifteen years before being suspended for excessive use of force. Mark, whose general philosophy of life is that it stinks, has been fired from his latest job, and initially rejects Jonathan's attempt at friendship. Mark thinks Jonathan is "too nice" and possibly a conman. To motivate the residents of Havencrest, who are doing little more than waiting to die, Jonathan engages them in helping to plant flowers and arranges for a picnic. Sid Gold (John Bleifer), a lonely man in love with Estelle, brings her flowers and tries to get her to join the festivities, but she refuses. Only Jonathan's dog motivates her to go outdoors. When Mark interrogates Jonathan about his lack of personal possessions and need of food, Jonathan reluctantly confesses he is an angel in training, and that he could use Mark's help. Mark calls him a kook, but changes his mind after Jonathan magically produces a steak that was not there before. Upon learning that Havencrest is going to be sold unless the residents can come up with $116,000 in one day, Mark suggests betting on a horse race at the Santa Anita track. The old folks' horse wins, but not before a clever turn of events. Jonathan tells Mark it is time for him to move on, and that his work gets lonely sometimes. Mark says, "I want to help you help people," but Jonathan says it is not his decision, and Mark drives off. The truck, however, stalls—Jonathan's sign that Mark is indeed destined to be his assistant.

Just as the topic of religion is muted (God usually referred to as a friend or The Boss), so are the displays of Jonathan's otherworldly gifts, such as his invulnerability, superhuman strength, knowledge of everything about people he has never met, ability to often predict the future, and creative methods of securing employment though he has no past. More substantial are his observations regarding humanity. Jonathan to Leslie: "Never underestimate the power of love." Jonathan to Mark: "It always amazes me how people who are so lonely, so devoid of love in their lives, still consider themselves successful." Jonathan to Mark: "Some people choose to be friends. Some choose to be strangers." Hinting at his own tragic past, Jonathan says to Sid: "A lot of people don't live long enough to get old."

Although the prospect of romance for Jonathan is moot, Landon is still able to effortlessly make the subject of love a central theme not only in the premiere episode, but throughout the entire series. Sid's pursuit of Estelle is a touching reminder that love has no age limit. The owner of Havencrest learns that a woman he once wanted to marry died while waiting for him to stop being wrapped up in his work, an admonition not to let love pass by. Leslie goes to clean Jonathan's room after he has gone, and discovers a new tenant—and possible romantic interest—already there.

As executive producer, Landon economized by using actual homes rather than constructing exterior or interior sets at MGM whenever possible, a trend starting with "To Touch the Moon" (09-26-84), the first regular episode and the first of nineteen (counting the two-hour premiere as two installments) he would both write and direct. Mark—wearing his Oakland A's cap that has seen better days, and uttering the first of his numerous "cute, Jonathan, cute" responses to his partner's use of the supernatural "stuff"—and Jonathan are assigned to unite Tony, a delinquent boy, and a widow whose son, Arthur, is dying of cancer. (Academy Award-nominated Carrie Snodgress guest stars as Evelyn Nealy, Arthur's mother.) Arthur Nealy is first shown in bed at night with hi space ship models, praying to live long enough to touch the moon, seen through a window from his point of view. When a doctor informs Evelyn that her son's disease is no longer in remission, and there is no need to begin treatments again, she breaks down. (Landon focuses on the doctor's reaction to how badly Evelyn takes the news rather than on how distraught she becomes.) Jonathan and Mark encounter Tony hitchhiking and pick him up, and the boy repays their kindness by stealing Mark's car. While Mark tracks Tony down, Jonathan shows up at Evelyn's house with a gift for Arthur, telling her he worked at NASA with her late husband, an astronaut who had walked on the moon. Remarking that everyone has given up on Tony—including the boy's parents—and Tony has given up on life, Mark takes him under his wing. Gradually, Arthur and Tony form a bond, as do Tony and Evelyn. In the hospital, waiting to die, Arthur tells his mother he is not afraid of dying, but that Tony is afraid of being alone. She promises he will not be alone. After Evelyn leaves, Jonathan shows up and asks Arthur if he is ready to go to the moon. Landon alternates shots of the camera moving in on the moon with shots of Arthur, who lifts his hand just before the moon fills the screen. "I touched it, Mr. Smith," the boy says. "I touched the moon!" To which Jonathan replies, "You're home, son. You're home."

Despite being a world famous television star, Landon was a "hands on" father who never lost touch with his blue collar roots, and championed the importance of strong family ties. After nearly three decades in the entertainment industry, he had doubtlessly witnessed or at least heard of the dysfunctional relationships all too common between show business parents and their offspring. Such observations no doubt led to his "Catch a Falling Star" (11-14-84), in which Jonathan and Mark's assignment involves mending fences between film star Lance Gaylord and his son, Brock. In addition to demonstrating that familial bonds should not be sacrificed in favor of work, Landon has the opportunity to show bratty child actors and stage mothers at their worst. As Jonathan Smith, he gets to catch a bullet in midair. The gunman, a junkie, cannot believe what he has seen, and swears he is never doing drugs again. Brock auditions for a role in one of his father's films, a Western being shot at Old Tucson, and the two of them communicate how they truly feel about one another by reciting lines in the script.

"Plane Death" (01-09-85), written by Landon and the third episode (of an eventual dozen) directed by Victor French, is a condemnation of the drug culture as well as one of the few moments of *Highway* heavy on action. Mark and Jonathan investigate the disappearance of one of Mark's law enforcement buddies and run into a motorcycle gang smuggling cocaine across the border into California via remote controlled model airplanes. After an altercation, Mark asks Jonathan why he did not use "the stuff," and is told it is not Jonathan's assignment, but it is Mark's problem. Not until the buried car of Mark's friend is discovered does "the Boss" instruct Jonathan to get involved. In a dramatic confrontation—highlighted by the sudden appearance of Jonathan silhouetted in the doorway of a darkened tavern, a storm raging behind him—Jonathan stands up to the gang and is, predictably, unharmed by a shotgun blast. When the gang attempts to escape on their motorcycles, the bikes will not start—thanks to "the stuff"—and the Feds swoop in to arrest them. Tragically, Mark's missing friend has been killed. He asks Jonathan if there will ever be a time when the country puts drugs away forever, and Jonathan says if not there might not be a country to wonder about.

Landon reached back into his archives again for "A Child of God" (01-06-85), a modern adaptation of his *Bonanza* script "The Love Child." Appropriately, David Rose's Emmy Award-winning music from that 1970 episode is reprised, effectively underscoring the familiar yet still potent story of a father disowning a daughter who has given birth out of wedlock and is dying. Landon manages to heighten the drama by making the father, David Stearns (William Windom), a judgmental minister. Stearns' daughter, Marsha, and her daughter, Amy, live in the same apartment building as Jonathan and Mark. After hearing about the trouble between Marsha and her father, Jonathan assures her she is not a sinner, because she loves Amy. "People who judge others rely on guilt," he says. "It keeps them from having to deal with their own feelings of guilt." Reverend Stearns tells Jonathan that Marsha is an adulteress unworthy of a second chance. Angry, Jonathan replies that Stearns' soul is the one in need of salvation, not Marsha's. The minister agrees to raise Amy, but does not soften toward Marsha until he learns she has only six months to live. At the conclusion, the camera moves in Marsha's smiling face as she sits in church listening to her father tell the congregation, "Spend your time on this earth loving, not judging." For his work on this episode, Ted Voigtlander received another Emmy nomination for Outstanding Cinematography for a Series.

Landon directed his teleplay for "A Match Made in Heaven" (02-20-85), based on a story by quadriplegic actor/writer James Troesh and his wife, Theresa. (James appears as attorney Scotty Wilson, a role he first played in the two-part installment "One Fresh Batch of Lemonade" in October.) A love story concerning the problematic courtship of Scotty and Mark's cousin, Diane, this episode illustrates perfectly Landon's belief that the disabled should not be treated differently than anyone else simply because they are handicapped. The final scene, a long shot of wheelchair-bound wedding guests cheering and waving as the van carrying Scotty and Diane drives away, is as life affirming as it gets. (Sadly, James Troesh passed away in October 2011 at the age 54.) Brianne Murphy's camerawork received an Emmy nomination for this episode.

A *Little House* reunion of sorts took place for "The Right Thing" (03-27-85), written by Landon, directed by French, and guest starring Matthew Laborteaux as Matt Haynes, a young man whose parents put his beloved grandfather, Harry (Lew Ayres), in a retirement home against the elderly man's wishes. Jonathan, working at the home, meets the despondent Harry, and tells Matt his grandfather needs to be active. Harry was once athletic, so his grandson brings him a new pair of walking shoes in an unsuccessful attempt to get him out into the world. According to Matt, Harry stopped living after the death of his wife. Jonathan appears in Harry's room—revealed in a mirror as Harry approaches it—and tells him to get off his butt and live. Harry calls Matt and says he wants to start walking. Later, Jonathan gives Harry a new pair of running shoes so Harry and

Matt can compete in a Granddad and Grandson Run. In the meantime, turmoil ensues at the Haynes house—Matt's father angry about Harry being put in a home, Matt's mother adamant that Harry stay there. Caught in the middle, Matt feels all the trouble is his fault. Jonathan tells him not to feel guilty, that "there's nothing wrong with helping a loved one." Unbeknown to Matt's mother, Ann, her husband, Jim, makes a bet with Harry that he can move back home if he wins the race, and when she learns of the deal she blows up. Harry and Matt triumph—their win depicted by showing the trophy in Harry's room rather than the actual race—and Ann follows through with her threat to pack up and leave her husband and son. Harry, however, announces he is going off on a trip to see everything he has never seen, and will get his own place when he returns. Instead of being harsh toward Ann, he tells her he understands how she feels. Matt tells his grandfather he loves him; Harry says he knows.

The second season of *Highway to Heaven* was its most successful, rising to #13 in the annual ratings. Its competition—*Stir Crazy* on CBS, *The Insiders* on ABC—did not stand a chance. Of the twenty-four episodes, Landon wrote four and directed all but eight, including "The Smile in the Third Row" (11-20-85), which reunited him with his longtime friend and *Bonanza* co-star Lorne Greene.

Ten years before, Landon told Greene there was an ideal guest part for him coming up on *Little House*, but that he could not have it. "Michael called and said if we worked together people would ask, 'Why doesn't he recognize his own father?'" Greene said. "He said he wanted me to know he was thinking of me." After more time had passed, and the two actors became less identified with their iconic Cartwright roles, Landon felt that a *Highway* story by Lan O'Kun, about a Broadway actor who claims he can see God seated in the audience, was perfect for Greene. "I knew that he would call me if the right thing came up," Greene said, "and he did. He sent me this strange, different and wonderful script. I read it and said, 'Yeah, I think that's the one.' It was marvelous working with Michael again, and a lot of the old crew from *Bonanza* was working with the show. It was like old home week." (The possibility for another Landon/Greene pairing presented itself when producer David Dortort asked them to step back into their Cartwright boots for a new telefilm, *Bonanza: The Next Generation*. Greene agreed, and Landon was allegedly considering the offer until Greene became seriously ill and had to back out. On September 11, 1987, on the eve of *Bonanza*'s twenty-eighth anniversary, Greene passed away. Landon, who had visited him the previous day, said, "He was Ben Cartwright to the end. I took his hand in mine and held it. He looked at me and slowly started to arm wrestle like we used to. Then he broke into a smile and nodded. And everything was okay. I think he wanted me to know everything was okay." The revival of Dortort's creation was released in syndication the following March, with Michael Landon, Jr., cast as Benj, the grandson of Ben Cartwright.)

In "Alone" (01-08-86), the first of four second season episodes both written and directed by Landon, Jonathan and Mark help Arnie, a mentally challenged homeless boy, find love and acceptance, and at the same time bring together a divorced couple. Similar to other Landon-penned stories, the outcome of the episode is fairly predictable, but as with life itself, the journey is more interesting than the destination. Viewers may well be more than reasonably certain Arnie will end up staying with the couple and their son. However, it is Landon's skill as a storyteller that captures the viewer's attention and makes the development of the episode more engaging, perhaps, than its conclusion, sprinkling appropriate social commentary—verbal and visual—along the way. Although Arnie's life changes for the good, Landon reminds the viewer that some things, unfortunately, remain unchanged by showing the same bum sitting in the same alley as the episode begins and as it ends.

Landon directed his script for "Keep Smiling" (02-05-86), a highlight of the series which reveals Jonathan's real name to be Arthur Thompson, and that he died in 1948, six months shy of his thirty-first birthday. Jonathan and Mark's assignment is none other than Jonathan's wife, Jane (Dorothy McGuire), feeling lonesome and neglected by her daughter, Mandy. While Jonathan cheers Jane up, Mark travels to Illinois to try convincing Mandy and her family to visit Los Angeles rather than take a Hawaiian vacation. Mark's efforts are futile, so Jonathan materializes on Mandy's porch pretending to be a younger, hip man (Don Johnson's character on *Miami Vice* would be an apt example) intent on marrying Jane. His obnoxious behavior shocks Mandy and her husband into deciding they must go see Jane and talk some sense into her. Jonathan and Mark drive off as a taxi drops Mandy and her family off at Jane's house. Mark stops the car, and Jonathan gets out, observing the reunion from a distance. As one would logically expect, the episode contains several memorable moments, chief among them Jonathan and Jane's fireside chat on the beach at night, during which she says that being with him is almost like being with Arthur again. (Earlier, he uses Arthur's slogan—"keep smiling"—and plays Claude Debussy's "Claire de Lune," Arthur's favorite piece of music, on the piano.) Jonathan replies that she reminds him of a woman he once loved a long time ago. "Never say goodbye," Jonathan tells her. "Say till we meet again." Landon would not disappoint viewers who hoped for a sequel.

"The Last Assignment" (02-12-86), an expert blend of comedy and drama written and directed by Landon, finds Jonathan and Mark attempting to rein in Harold (Edward Asner), an angel who has been on probation for 200 years, longer than any other. Harold, dressed as Santa Claus, gives money away and dispenses wine from a fire hydrant, much to the delight of the local derelicts. Jonathan explains to him that an angel is supposed to help people, and give them love and understanding, not simply give them things. When Harold says he is not good at getting people to help themselves, Jonathan suggests they team up and help each other out. Although guiding Harry results in a number of amusing scenes, it is Harry who helps a minister regain his faith. As Jonathan and Mark drive out of town, they hear on the car radio that Harry has won three million dollars in the lottery and is giving it away to people who need it. Mark slams on the brakes and turns the car around.

The second season ended with Landon writing and directing "Friends" (05-07-86), an episode about the rite of passage known as high school, specifically the various traumas that can occur there. Jonathan and Mark hire on as substitute teachers, Jonathan teaching math and English, and Mark, to his embarrassment, sex education. Jenny Bates, an overweight student with an eating compulsion, is not happy when Jonathan assigns an essay on the subject "What a Friend Means to Me"—she has no friends. Her life is complicated further when Jonathan asks her to tutor Jack, an athlete whose grades are suffering and on whom Jenny has a crush. When she refuses to cheat for him, Jack fails a test and is kicked off the team. He blames Jonathan and challenges him to a fight, which Jack loses. Jenny asks Jonathan to give Jack one more chance, but Jack wants nothing to do with Jenny until he learns that she is the one who feels he should have another opportunity to pass. Happily, Jack's academic record improves, as does his relationship with Jenny, but this rosy scenario is threatened by Arlene, Jack's girlfriend. Arlene invites Jenny to join a girl's club, and at an alleged initiation party, has her put on a small bathing suit. When Jack arrives, thinking he is picking Arlene up for a date, Arlene and the other girls push Jenny into a room with Jack and will not let her out. Jack tells Arlene she is sick, and Jenny, humiliated, puts on a coat and drives off to her favorite haunt, the local donut shop. There, Jonathan tells Jenny that Jack called and told him what happened. The best friend she has, Jonathan says, is herself, and that she has to love herself first. He drives her home, where Jack is waiting. Jack declares that if he can pass algebra, she can lose weight. "What do you say—friend?" he asks.

Highway to Heaven returned for a third season on September 24, 1986, dropping to tie with ABC's *Dynasty* at #24 in the year-end ratings, but still winning its Wednesday night time slot opposite sitcoms on both of the other networks. Landon wrote four and directed all but three of the twenty-five episodes. (One of only three he neither wrote nor directed, "That's Our Dad," nevertheless contained a dig at one of his favorite targets—the *National Enquirer*—and a reference to someone dying after ordering a bowl of soup, just as his father had done.)

Landon's love of animals, dogs in particular, resulted in a high point of the series, "For the Love of Larry" (10-08-86), which he both wrote and directed. The basic plot has a dog, Boomer, desperately trying to get someone to follow him to where a man and his son lie injured in a car wreck. Complications and delays ensue, of course, but Landon comes up with a surprise ending guaranteed to burst the tear ducts of anyone who finds it emotionally draining to watch Disney's *Old Yeller*. When Mark tells Boomer's owner that the dog is responsible for him and his son being found, the man says it is impossible—Boomer died in the crash. A policeman remarks that it was a miracle the accident victims were found, figuring the dog must have been a look-alike. He asks Jonathan if he wants help finding the dog, to which Jonathan replies, "No, I have a feeling he's probably home by now." The camera pulls up from the demolished vehicle, through the trees and into the sky, where Boomer's image is superimposed against the clouds. The episode is not without its lighter moments, such as when Mark mistakenly believing that he suddenly possesses "the stuff" and is impervious to bullets. Landon fans will note that two characters, Chris and Shawna, are named after two of his children.

In "Wally" (01-14-87), written and directed by Landon, the spotlight is on guest star Dick Van Dyke in an Emmy-worthy role as the title character, a homeless man who ekes out a living by entertaining pedestrians with a pair of marionettes, one of them a bum. He shares his meager income with fellow street people, and lives in a railroad boxcar with a crippled dog he calls Long John Silver. Jonathan and Mark, dressed as destitute men for their assignment, join Wally on his daily rounds, which include visiting the home of Stevie, a dying boy, and putting on a show. When Wally offers to give Long John Silver to Stevie, the boy says it would not be a good idea because the dog will most likely outlive him. Wally claims to be an angel, and when Stevie asks what Heaven will be like, he tells him. Wally has also been staging performances at an old folks' home three times a week for three years. One of the residents, a former homeless person named Sylvia, has suffered a stroke, but Wally and his friends pay for her keep. Jonathan tells Mark that Wally, because of his selflessness, really could be an angel. When Margaret, an alcoholic acquaintance who feels she is worthless, is shot and killed in a liquor store holdup, Wally holds her in his arms and recites the Lord's Prayer. (Van Dyke nailed the scene in one take.) The next time the trio visits Stevie, they discover he is in a coma and being taken to the hospital. There, Jonathan says he is a doctor, and when asked why he is dressed like a bum, replies that it is because he does not overcharge his patients. Wally prays for God to take him instead of Stevie. When Mark asks, Jonathan confirms that Wally's time is up. That night Wally is shot outside a liquor store, but the shooting is only heard. Instead, Landon shows the bum marionette lying on the sidewalk as if dead. In the ambulance, Jonathan admits to being an angel, and tells

Wally that his prayer for Stevie to recover will come true because Wally has been an angel all of his life. The camera zeroes in on a monitor flat lining, and the paramedic misjudges Wally as "just a bum who wasted his life." At the hospital, Stevie's monitor begins to signal an improvement in his condition, and a nurse informs his parents that he is out of his coma. Jonathan and Mark go to Stevie's house to deliver Long John Silver, and the boy's mother tells them a miracle has occurred—all of her son's cancer is gone. Stevie says that Wally is in the room telling him he is going on a long trip and is in a hurry. Left behind, for Stevie, is Wally's bum marionette.

More a quarter-century has passed since Landon's "The Hero" (02-18-87), an episode detailing an ex-soldier's frustrating experience with the Veteran's Administration, and little, unfortunately, has changed. James Stacy, former star of television's *Lancer* and who lost an arm and a leg in a 1973 motorcycle accident, portrays veteran Joe Mason. Government red tape has prevented him from receiving badly needed dental care, estimated to be $3800, and during his fourth appointment with VA officials he is told he is not entitled to any benefits "in this instance" because his condition is not connected to his time in the service. Joe becomes agitated, asks the VA board to review his case again, and goes to a bar instead of returning to his job as a bank teller. While drinking he hears a television report about a convicted killer receiving dental work. Jonathan, also employed as a teller, joins him for lunch. Joe is offended when a customer pays his tab, assuming it is only because he is a disabled vet. Angry, he says he does need pity, just to be treated the same as murderers and thieves. Joe lies to his wife, telling her he has straightened things out with the VA. Jonathan accompanies him to his dentist, Doctor Bonner, who informs Joe that the VA is still denying coverage. After Jonathan and Mark tell Joe's wife the truth about the situation, she asks her husband why he lied, why he will not share what he is going through. Joe says he is going to get a loan for the dental work, but steals the money instead. Jonathan, in an effort to convince Joe he is a hero, with nothing to prove, contacts a vet whose life Joe saved, and has him come to the bank. Witnessing Joe's theft, Jonathan asks him if he really believes he is going to get away with the crime, and tells him that it is no way to be a hero. His wife does not love him because she needs him,

Jonathan adds—she needs him because she loves him. Joe puts the money back, but remarks that the government still owes him. Jonathan, who agrees that the system stinks, says, "You're damn right, they do."

In "Heavy Date" (03-18-87), Landon's fourth and final episode as writer and director for the third season, Jonathan and Mark are tasked with uniting Alice (still one of Landon's favorite character names), a pregnant and unmarried woman, and Gary, an irresponsible young man. (In a biographical reference, Landon characterizes Gary's mother as a bit of a loon who, like Landon's mother, puts her head in the oven not once, but twice.) Alice rents an apartment in the building owned by Gary's mother, and where Jonathan and Mark happen to reside. When a drunken Gary crashes his car and hurts his head, Jonathan and Mark deposit him outside Alice's door. She lets him in to wash his injury. The following day, Alice sees a doctor who tells her the pregnancy is going well, and she tells him she still intends to put the baby up for adoption. Her mother knows about her condition, but her father thinks she is in Europe. Returning home, she discovers a dinner invitation from Gary on her answering machine. Jonathan says Gary is a good person who has not found the right person. (During a scene depicting the young couple's growing relationship, director Landon inserts a visual symbol of Alice's impending delivery by showing a plant whose buds are about to open.) Gary tells Alice he loves her, but when she reveals that she is seven months pregnant, he walks out without uttering a word. Jonathan asks him if he loves Alice, to which he replies that he did, but not now. Gary cannot base a relationship on something someone did before they met, Jonathan lectures him, adding, "If you love her, don't throw it away because of ego or false pride." Alice and Gary reconcile, and she tells him the baby's father ran out on her. Then her judgmental father shows up, saying she is no longer fooling him about her situation. After he leaves, Alice tells Gary she feels sorry for her father, that he seemed so pathetic. Gary calls him a jerk, promising to be there for her as much as she wants. Although it is clear the story is headed toward a positive end, writer Landon manages to delay the inevitable by keeping the adoption only a possibility until the final moments. Jonathan helps convince Gary to propose to Alice by prodding him to look at her newborn boy. Drawing inspiration from his unbalanced mother, Gary scares the adopting couple—who believe him to be the biological father—by telling them that his father abandoned him when his mother went nuts, and mental trouble runs in his family. Kneeling beside Alice's bed, he asks her to marry him, saying, "You're mine—and he's mine." Gary asks Jonathan to break the news to his mother, as it might be easier for her to take coming from a stranger. Mark, who gets along with the woman, gets the job, and she reacts by putting her head in the oven.

Highway to Heaven dropped out of the Top 30 programs during its fourth season, its second half-hour scheduled at the same time as ABC's *Head of the Class*, the most popular show on Wednesday evening and #23 in the year-end tally. Ratings, however, were not Landon's top priority. He continued to pour his creative energy into making the production as vital and relevant as ever, directing all twenty-four episodes and writing five, including a two-part installment many admirers consider the best of the series. Among the guest stars were Hollywood legends Donald O'Connor ("Playing for Keeps") and Bob Hope ("Heaven Nose, Mr. Smith").

For the premiere episode, the two-part "Man's Best Friend" (09-16/23-87), Jonathan and Mark return to the boarding kennel first seen in the previous season's "For the Love of Larry" to handle dogs used for visiting days at a retirement home and an orphanage. Although Jonathan tells Mark he cannot understand the exact purpose of their assignment, it gradually develops that a runaway dog is the catalyst for bringing together a lonely orphan boy and a well-to-do family (the father played by *Little House*'s Stan Ivar) whose surrogate has lost the baby. On the surface a straightforward tale, yet Landon succeeds in sustaining interest across both parts by injecting unexpected plot twists and clever touches of humor: Searching for the lost dog, Jonathan scares away a trio of coyotes by transforming himself into a lion. When Jonathan tells Mark their assignment is not over until the fat lady sings, Landon cuts to an opera singer belting out an aria in an old movie on television. After the wealthy couple agrees to adopt the orphan boy, who has befriended their dog, Mark says he knows now why dogs are man's best friend. Jonathan replies, "You'd think man's best friend would be man."

One of the most memorable episodes of the series is "I Was a Middle-Aged Werewolf" (10-28-87), a Halloween story that aired three days before the holiday, also Landon's birthday. Writer/director Landon has the proverbial field day spoofing his infamous 1957 role, going so far as to be made up as the titular beast, snarling and terrorizing Mark in two sequences. (Hank Edds, Michael Westmore and Gerald Quist all received Emmy nominations for Outstanding Achievement in Makeup for a Series.) Opening with eerie music and a shot of clouds scuttling across the moon, Jonathan and Mark drive along and reminisce about Halloween, accompanied by a flashback to the second season's "The Devil and Jonathan Smith" (10-30-85). They stop at a shop called Satan's Subs so Mark can order a Devil's Delight, a sandwich served by Satan himself (from the earlier episode) disguised in a human mask. In their hotel room, Mark watches *I Was a Teenage Werewolf* on the late show, remarking that the lead actor looks a lot like Jonathan. Warning Mark that the sandwich is going to give him bad dreams, Jonathan goes out for a walk. Alan, a young trick-or-treater who has been fooled into believing his sister and a friend are in danger, has his candy stolen by two older boys. Jonathan shows up and tells them to return the candy, but they put the treat bag over his head. When he removes it, he has turned into a werewolf. Alan's tormentors run. The boy says that his sister and a friend have been grabbed by a man, but when Jonathan investigates he learns it is a hoax. At the hotel, Mark falls asleep and dreams that Jonathan has become a werewolf, and the policeman he calls is also one. Jonathan returns and wakes him up. Mark insists that the kid in the movie really did resemble Jonathan. "Mark," he replies, "I was never that young." Alan's mother orders her husband to look for their son. The father, who declined to take Alan trick-or-treating, considers the boy a sissy. Alan confides in Jonathan, telling him that his father is tough and has never cried. Jonathan helps Alan get back at his sister and her friend by turning into a werewolf and pretending to be scared off when the boy confronts him. Alan's father is about the call the police for help in finding his son when Alan returns and apologizes for disappearing. His father breaks down and cries for the first time. Jonathan goes back to the hotel and transforms himself into a werewolf to scare Mark and, as in his friend's dream, becomes a policeman who is also a werewolf. Landon looks directly at the camera, winks and says, "Happy Halloween." The camera freezes on the werewolf's "smiling" features.

Just as *Bonanza*'s "Forever" and *Little House*'s "The Lord is My Shepherd" and "Remember Me" have emerged as Landon's undeniable masterpieces from his earlier series, so too has Highway's two-part "We Have Forever" (02-10/17-88) become recognized as a definite highlight of his career. Significantly, it is the Jonathan Smith's most personal story since season two's "Keep Smiling," to which this episode is a sequel. It begins typically enough, with Mark complaining to Jonathan, this time about crooked television evangelists. Jonathan replies, "Power changes people, Mark. Religion and politics are great places to gain that power." As they drive along Jonathan thinks he has heard something but decides it must have been his imagination. The scene cuts to a hospital corridor, then the room of Jane Thompson (Dorothy McGuire), Jonathan's wife. She mutters his name twice. In the car, he tells Mark he hears her, and that she is dying. Jonathan appears at her bedside, the familiar strains of Debussy's "Claire de Lune" playing on the soundtrack. He speaks her name, and she looks up, the only light in the darkened room that which illuminates their faces. Jane is scared, but Jonathan tells her there is no need to be afraid. She wants to know if she is going to see her husband Arthur again. He says yes. As in the earlier episode, she remarks that he reminds her of Arthur, it is in his eyes. Jane has tears in hers, but smiles and, before dying, tells him she is no longer fearful. Jonathan kisses her forehead and says, "I love you, Jane Thompson." He tells Mark she is gone, and that he expects he will be Heaven-bound before the night is out, that there is no reason for him to stay now that Jane has died. Mark is understandably upset. The two friends go to the beach after sundown and reminisce, Mark admitting that being with Jonathan and helping people have given him the best years of his life. Jonathan tells him to keep helping people, hears something, and announces he has to be alone. He walks away and suddenly shouts, "No—I won't! I won't!" The sky is filled with lightning and thunder. "I won't!" he repeats. "I did my best for forty years! No more! I'm through!" Pushing Mark away, he warns his friend, "You don't want to be with me anymore!" On a busy street Jonathan spots a theater marquee advertising the film

Heaven Can Wait. He smashes a liquor store window, starts grabbing bottles and throwing them at the marquee. The police arrest him, and when Mark bails him out there is an injury on his face. Jonathan reveals that the Boss has taken away "the stuff." All he wants to do is get drunk. He tells Mark their partnership is over, that being good, kind and loving does not amount to anything. Returning to the beach by himself, Jonathan tells the Boss he will not say he is sorry for his actions until he gets to see Jane again. He spots a woman alone in the distance. Believing it is Jane, he calls her name, but when he realizes it is not her, says, "Sorry, I thought you were someone else." The woman, whom he later learns is named Jennifer Sims, walks slowly into the ocean. Jonathan rescues her, opens her purse to find her address, and takes her home. The following morning, he tells her he has lost a job he had been at for forty years. Jennifer says he does not look old enough to have been working that long. She confesses that a longtime love broke their engagement without a word and disappeared six months ago. Before leaving, Jonathan says her fiancé does not sound like someone worth killing herself over, advising her to get angry instead. As he walks down the highway, Jennifer pulls up in her car and offers him a ride, admitting that she was lonesome after he left. He tells her he had an argument with his boss, but does not miss the job. She reveals her source of income to be a trust fund. When she suddenly stops and darts into traffic, Jonathan thinks she is making another suicide attempt, but she is going after a small dog that has been struck by a hit and run driver. After a veterinarian has tended to the animal, Jennifer invites Jonathan to move in with her. In the meantime, Mark feels adrift without his partner, and turns down a job offer from the head of a school for the blind where he and Jonathan worked (in the 11-18-87 episode "All the Colors of the Heart"). Jonathan makes a cart with wheels for the hindquarters of the rescued dog, which he and Jennifer name Ewe. He confesses that she reminds him of his late wife, that he would like to hold her but feels guilty. The anger he once felt is gone now that he has met her. She says he has a great deal of love in his soul, and it is wrong for him to let guilt or anger take its place. Following a flashback to Jonathan and Jane talking on the beach in "Keep Smiling," he looks up to the sky and tells Jane that Jennifer reminds him of her, he needs to feel love again, please try to understand. He and Jennifer go to dinner in a restaurant where she asks the pianist to play her favorite piece, "Claire de Lune." Jonathan says it was also his wife's favorite, and that it is the only song he knows how to play. While his attempts to find a job are unsuccessful, Mark is working in a warehouse and hates it. He has been late three mornings in a row, thinks nothing of goofing off by spending time goofing around with a bubble maker. (Cue the theme from *The Lawrence Welk Show* on the soundtrack.) Predictably, he is fired and accepts the position at the blind school, Camp Laurelbrook, after all. A frustrated Jonathan tells Jennifer praying is a waste of time, but she does not buy it, adding that she has prayed they will be together forever. He walks down to the water at night and, with tears in his eyes, asks for forgiveness. (The camera swings slowly around to show Jennifer watching him from the deck of the house.) The next day, she seems sad but tells Jonathan she is going to run some errands and has a surprise for supper. Instead, she drives to Camp Laurelbrook and informs a puzzled Mark that Jonathan is ready for more assignments. She hands him a letter to give to Jonathan at a certain market. Back home, she tells Jonathan she forgot to buy butter and asks him to get some. Before he leaves, she makes a point of saying she loves him. Jonathan and Mark have a joyful reunion outside the market. Mark hands Jennifer's letter to Jonathan which reveals, in not so many words, that she is also an angel. The letter is signed, Jane. They drive back to Jennifer's house, only to discover a vacant lot. Jonathan says he is fine now—they have an assignment. The camera slowly moves in on the waves crashing on the beach.

Cast as Jennifer Sims was Leann Hunley, who was currently portraying Dana Waring Carrington on ABC's nighttime soap *Dynasty*, but was said to be tiring of the role. A couple of months after "We Have Forever" aired, a tabloid reported that in an effort to reverse *Highway*'s decline in the ratings, Landon was planning to bring Hunley back as a regular in the fifth season. Not only that, the characters of Jonathan/Arthur and Jennifer/Jane were going to be married. As fans of the series know, this development never occurred.

In June NBC announced that due to diminishing popularity, the next season of *Highway to Heaven* would be its last. Landon agreed to produce thirteen more episodes, but the network did faithful viewers no favors by airing them erratically in October (one episode), December (two episodes), March (one episode) and the remaining nine (on Friday rather than the customary Wednesday timeslot) during the summer of 1989. Landon wrote the final episode and directed all thirteen. The June 16 episode, "The Squeaky Wheel," written by Paul W. Cooper, includes the amusing scene where Jonathan and Mark come across Michael Landon's star on the Hollywood Walk of Fame, placed there on August 15, 1984:

MARK: Oh, here's another one of my favorites—Michael Landon. (Takes photo)

JONATHAN: Never heard of him.

MARK: Are you kidding? *Bonanza, Little House on the Prairie*...

JONATHAN: Sorry—doesn't ring a bell.

MARK: I keep forgetting—you've been dead for 40 years.

Tragically, Victor French became ill with lung cancer shortly after wrapping the final season the previous fall. On June 7, he was admitted to Sherman Oaks Community Hospital. "He's the best man a friend could have," Landon said. "My whole family adores him. I can't bear to see him suffer. I can't believe this is happening." Appropriately, the June 9 episode (not June 16, as has been stated in some sources) was followed by a special written message to French from the cast and crew. Six days later, one of Landon's few genuinely close friends in the industry was gone at the age of 54. "The Squeaky Wheel" aired the following night.

The last episode of *Highway to Heaven*, "Merry Christmas from Grandpa" (08-04-89), was Landon's grim update of the classic *A Christmas Carol*. A cautionary tale, Jonathan and Mark warn three men, including the President of the United States, of the dangers posed by nuclear energy and chemical pollution. There are timely references to the disasters at Three Mile Island and the ill-fated space shuttle Challenger, as well as visions of a future where people die from the effects of water poisoned by nuclear waste and toxic chemicals, and fight over what little fresh water remains. In the White House, the president and the first lady are visited by several children wearing robes and carrying candles while singing "Silent Night." Jennifer, Landon's youngest daughter, calls the president "great, great, great, great, great Grandfather." Jonathan says these are the great grandchildren the president *would* have had if he had been able to prevent world destruction. When the president protests that he cannot stop it by himself, Jonathan replies that it is everyone's responsibility to bring about peace. With that message, *Highway to Heaven* came to an end.

In May, shortly before the last nine episodes were broadcast, Landon waxed philosophically about the nature of long-running shows: "I think a lot of it has to do with probably picking the right material, first of all, and a great deal of it has to do with luck. You have to get the right timeslot. The ideas I've had for series have never been ones the networks, generally, have embraced immediately."

Looking back at the series a year later, Landon told television talk show host Larry King: "I got a lot of flak from a lot of various people, even on religious shows on television. I was called Satan, the Devil. Only because I did not preach the Gospel exactly the way they would like to hear it."

As the sole owner of *Highway to Heaven*, Landon personally handled the marketing of the series in reruns, supervising the editing of the episodes (to allow for more commercials in syndication) so that none of the story elements were lost, as so frequently occurs when independent stations broadcast shows after their network runs are over. These versions were the first released on home video, but Mill Creek Entertainment has since issued the episodes on DVD uncut.

In 1994, CBS revived the spirit of *Highway* with *Touched by an Angel*, which had a successful life (Top 30 for five of its nine seasons), and even spawned a less popular spin off, *Promised Land* (three seasons), proving there was still an audience for something other than mindless action, prime time soap operas and inane sitcoms. Yet, all of these years later, *Highway to Heaven* is the thoughtful, inspirational series by which all others of its kind will forever be measured. And, no doubt, be found wanting. That may well also be true of the "edgier reboot" of *Highway* the A&E cable network currently has in development.

Chapter 8
The End
Where Pigeons Go to Die
(01-29-90)
Us
(09-20-91)

Landon on location for *Where Pigeons Go To Die*, 1990.
Robert Hy Gorman and Art Carney in background

> "I'm kind of old-fashioned in that I believe that a man's name is his real legacy to his children—his character, the way he's lived his life. Has he been fair? Has he been honest with people? I'd like to be remembered as an honest guy, a fair guy, that I've tried. I didn't try 100% all of the time because nobody does, but a good percentage"
>
> Michael Landon, 1990

During the fall of 1989, Landon and his crew spent time in four Kansas communities filming *Where Pigeons Go to Die*, based on the 1978 novel by R. Wright Campbell, and suggested to Landon by *Little House*'s Melissa Sue Anderson. "I just read a book that's really your cup of tea," she told him, and he agreed, electing to write and direct the project himself, with Anderson attached as one of the associate producers. NBC requested the title be changed to something more dynamic, but Landon refused. "I just wouldn't do it," he said, "because I think the author is entitled to have the same title on the film version. That's not a control battle—it's doing the right thing."

The film, beautifully photographed by longtime Landon associate Haskell "Buzzy" Boggs, is a moving meditation on life and death, punctuated by several thoughtful voice-overs by Landon taken directly from Campbell's novel. At its core, the story concerns the relationship between Hugh, a young boy of ten, and his grandfather, whom Hugh calls Da, who raise and race homing pigeons. The efforts of a bird named Dickens to surmount several obstacles during a return flight are juxtaposed with Da's struggle to recover from a stroke and go home. Bookending the film are scenes of a fifty-year-old Hugh (Landon) visiting the ramshackle remains of Da's house and pigeon coop, then walking toward the restored property as a grandfather himself, a grandson at his side.

Starring as Da was Art Carney, whose masterful performance earned him an Emmy nomination as Outstanding Lead Actor in a Miniseries or Special. (He lost out to Hume Cronyn in HBO's *Age-Old Friends*. Had he won, it would have been his seventh Emmy.) Landon's award was simply the opportunity to work with one of his all-time favorite people, whom he regarded as "an amazingly honest actor." "Believe me," he said, "when you meet Art Carney you're not disappointed. He's everything you'd want Art Carney to be." After production wrapped, Landon wrote the older thespian a thank you note saying that their working together was one of the most memorable experiences of his life. Regarding his performance, Carney said, "I'll tell you what inspired me—two words: Michael Landon. When you're connected with something with Michael Landon's name on it, you've got a class act.

Landon fills *Where Pigeons Go to Die* with numerous emotional touches: Adult Hugh has kept a carved peach seed given to him by

Da forty years before, and finds a wheel from a wagon he got for his tenth birthday—and which he later used to carry Da home from the hospital. In a wordless scene, when Hugh's father gives the hospitalized Da a shave with an electric razor, Da raises his chin to make the task easier, and Hugh's father smiles, then begins to weep. After getting out of the hospital after a second stroke, Da sleeps on his front porch with a photograph of him and his late wife in their youth. Landon even manages to make Dickens as beloved a character as any puppy or kitten, dramatizing the bird's ordeal in a series of incidents that are more suspenseful than one might expect.

The film is not without its moments of humor: As an inside joke, Landon names the agent from Jason Realty Dennis Korn, in real life his business manager. ("Michael did that to embarrass me," says Korn.) At a funeral service for one of Da's friends, a crying woman blows her nose through a dark veil. The man who throws a can at a yowling cat and tells it to shut up is none other than Landon's longtime production partner Kent McCray.

Shortly before *Where Pigeons Go to Die* aired, Landon remarked, "I have a better attitude about my work. I'm not as upset looking at it the first time as I used to be. First time in my life I've felt that way. I'm not as hard on myself anymore. Let's face it—this business is a lot of fun. I'm pretty lucky."

Landon may have developed an upbeat outlook regarding his work, but his opinion of NBC, his creative home for three decades, was another matter. *Pigeons* garnered positive reviews and a high rating, yet no one from the network called to congratulate Landon for having produced such an excellent film. Consequently, he decided it was time to move on. "I left NBC with no bad feeling toward anyone in the entertainment division," he said, emphasizing that he still considered Brandon Tartikoff—who had believed in *Highway to Heaven* when no one else did—"a good guy and a good friend. The problem was with business affairs. Rudeness. My business manager, who was also my friend, deserved respect and didn't receive it."

* * *

Although it was reported that he was thinking of starring in a sitcom, Landon's next project, produced for CBS, was one that had been simmering on the back burner since the final days of *Little House* in 1982. "A few years ago I had an idea for a show similar to *Highway to Heaven*," he said in 1985, as *Highway* was nearing the end of its first season. "It was about a writer who'd been in prison and hadn't seen the world for 15 years. A magazine sends him out to look at the world from a new perspective. But I couldn't do that today. I don't think people would accept anyone wanting to get that involved in other people's lives. People want to remain detached. There's so much fear now. People would look at you funny if you're friendly on the street."

At the time Landon felt that audiences would be more open to the idea of an angel "taking an interest in people." However, by 1989 he had reconsidered the concept of an ex-con reentering society as a roving reporter, resulting in US, the two-hour pilot for his fourth series. Like *Highway*, Landon's character would not be tied down to one location, and story ideas were virtually unlimited—*Route 66* with a van rather than a Corvette.

After 18 years in prison, Jeff Hayes (Landon), an aspiring writer, is cleared of crimes (robbery and murder) he did not commit and is released. Ellen, the woman with whom Jeff had a son, Cary, reveals that she is married and has two daughters. (One named Shawna, after one of Landon's daughters, and the other portrayed by his real-life daughter Jennifer, now a successful actor. A cab driver is played by the late Mark Landon.) Jeff asks how Cary is, and Ellen says the boy has graduated from high school and believes that his father was killed in an accident. Jeff goes to a seedy apartment building for an uncomfortable reunion with his father (*Seinfeld*'s Barney Martin), who believed Jeff was guilty. Nor is the relationship between Cary (Casey Peterson) and his stepfather, Paul (David Spielberg), much better. Conflict is the essence of drama, and Landon introduces even more in the person of Liz, a prostitute estranged from her mother, who tells Jeff, "Everybody needs someone who cares about them. There's nothing worse than being alone." After Liz is murdered, Jeff learns that her mother will not claim the body. Now employed as a reporter for the son of the man responsible for sending him to prison, he says he will pay for her burial. Jeff also comes to the aid of Cary, who has been drinking and getting in trouble, and reveals that he is the boy's father. Cary agrees to join Jeff in his adventures as a traveling journalist, and meets the grandfather he did not know he had. As Jeff watches his son and father embrace, the camera pulls away and up, the scene dissolving to a close-up of a typewriter banging out "US By Jeff Hayes."

The title has a double meaning, of course, referring to the three Hayes men as well as the United States, which, sadly, went unexplored in what surely would have been yet another heartfelt Landon creation. One wonders, for instance, what Jeff Hayes might have said about gay marriage, the war on terror, the divisive political climate of the country, immigration, drug cartels, global warming, or an increasingly self-absorbed and narcissistic society that relies more on texting and tweeting than live contact. Perhaps more than any other television personality, Landon's beliefs were expressed by his work, and one can be more than reasonably certain that through *Us* he would have continued to share his insights into the human condition.

US aired on September 20, 1991, nearly three months after Landon passed away.

* * *

Just as this has not been a book about the private life of Michael Landon, it is also not a detailed report of the circumstances surrounding his death. He succumbed to pancreatic and liver cancer on July 1, 1991, four months shy of what would have been his fifty-fifth birthday. In the past, he had sometimes confided to friends that he had a feeling he was going to die young, yet he was determined fight back and consider every avenue of treatment. After being diagnosed, he wisely held a press conference on April 8 during which he said, "If you're going to go on, if you're going to try to beat something, you're not going to do it standing in the corner." Disclosing his compromised health in his own words was an effort to counteract the invasive and lurid speculation he knew the tabloids would soon be spewing. The outpouring of support and sympathy he received from his family, friends and fans was unprecedented, resulting in seemingly endless phone calls and literally thousands of cards and letters. One month later, May 9, he bravely offered to appear on his friend Johnny Carson's *Tonight Show*, receiving a standing ovation from the studio audience before joking about the various treatments he was undergoing, and blasting the tabloids that, predictably, had wasted no time sensationalizing and distorting the facts of Landon's condition. It was his last public appearance. In a nine-page cover story for the June issue of *Life* magazine, he shared his final thoughts with reporter Brad Darrach, saying, "I'm going to survive if I can. If I can't, I'll know I fought the good fight. Look, there's only two things that can happen. I can win or I can lose. And I can handle both."

TV Guide, a publication Landon had an occasionally contentious relationship with, devoted respectful back-to-back cover stories on him for the weeks of July 13 and 20. Over the course of his career, he was featured on the cover of the magazine 22 times—including ten as Joe Cartwright—second only to Lucille Ball, with 29 covers to her credit.

On September 17, NBC aired a two-hour tribute to Landon, *Memories of Laughter and Love*, directed by Michael Landon, Jr., who in recent years has become a talented writer and director himself. "My father left us with a legacy we will cherish from one generation to the next," he said. "His shows touched our hearts, our souls and our minds. He taught us the value of life and the importance of family." (In May of 1999 CBS showed the controversial *Michael Landon: The Father I Knew*, starring John Schneider, co-written and directed by Landon Jr. The autobiographical account of his troubled youth in the shadow of a celebrity may have been well-intentioned in his view, but as David Dortort remarked, "I thought he was a little rough on his father.")

Landon had his detractors, just as everyone does, but to the people who knew him best, there were few people better. According to the late Barney Martin, Landon felt sorry for his fellow actors, not himself, when it was obvious that *Us* would never become a series. "I've been on a lot of sets where there's turmoil and such," Martin said. "But on Michael's set there was always just calmness and wonderfulness. It was just marvelous to be with him. He had wholesome, wonderful shows. The thing they gave the storyline, always, was he offered hope. I just can't tell you how I miss him."

Little House and *Father Murphy* star Merlin Olsen, who with Melissa Gilbert presented a tribute to Landon during the 1992 Emmy Awards ("Michael Landon: The Celebration of a Lifetime"), later said, "Michael made you feel more than anything. He had a wonderful sense of getting to our emotional core."

That sentiment was echoed by his *Little House* co-star, Karen Grassle: "He was wired into the American heartland, and he knew what people needed to hear about, what they needed to laugh at, and what they needed to cry about."

Landon was inducted into the Television Hall of Fame in October 1995. Prior to bringing the Landon family to the stage to accept the award, actor Patrick Duffy said, "If Michael Landon had an enemy it was indecision. His advice was: 'Do it.' Whatever you want to do, do it now. There are only so many tomorrows. He had many projects still on the table, but what he gave us is a bounty of timeless gifts, a legacy of television movies and series that obviously will stand the test of time."

Nearly a decade after Landon's passing, his loyal right-hand man, Kent McCray, recalled, "Michael enjoyed directing more than anything. He liked the creativity of directing and going on the set and working with the actors, working with the crew. He really enjoyed that. He liked to write, but felt it was a very lonely profession. He liked acting the least. But he was smart enough to know that the actors get the money. He meant an awful lot to a lot of people. There will never be another one like him. Never. He was genuine. He cared for people. The sweetest man I've ever known."

Shortly before Landon's death, the community center in Malibu, California, was named in his honor. One year later, the Los Angeles Oncologic Institute and St. Vincent Medical Center announced that a new cancer prevention center opening in the fall would also be named for him. Landon, his wife Cindy revealed, grew very concerned with what caused cancer, and what could be done to detect it. "He became more and more curious as to how it could be detected," she said, "and, ultimately, prevented."

Alex Sharp, a stuntman on *Bonanza* whose subsequent writing career was encouraged by Landon, remembered his mentor with affection: "When you think about it, he conquered the whole world. And I know there were people at NBC who hated his guts, because they wanted to see him fail. And he didn't fail. When we lost him in this town with a lot of baloney talent, he was the real thing, and God love him, wherever he is."

"Live every minute, guys."
Michael Landon (April 8, 1991)

The End

BIBLIOGRAPHY

BOOKS

Anderson, Melissa. *The Way I See It: A Look Back at My Life on Little House.* Guilford, CT: Globe Pequot Press, 2010.

Arngrim, Alison. *Confessions of a Prairie Bitch: How I Survived Nellie Oleson and Learned to Love Being Hated.* New York: HarperCollins Publishers, 2010.

Brooks, Tim and Earle Marsh. *The Complete Directory to Prime Time Network and Cable TV Shows 1946—Present: 20th Anniversary Edition.* New York: Ballantine Books, 1996.

Burlingame, Jon. *TV's Biggest Hits: The Story of Television Themes From "Dragnet" to Friends."* New York: Shirmer Books, 1996.

Flynn, Harry and Pamela Flynn. *Michael Landon: Life, Love & Laughter.* Universal City, CA: Pomegranate Press, Ltd., 1991.

Gilbert, Melissa. *Prairie Tale: A Memoir.* New York: Spotlight Entertainment/Simon & Schuster, Inc., 2009.

Greenland, David. *Bonanza: A Viewer's Guide to the TV Legend.* Albany, GA: BearManor Media, 2010.

Ito, Tom. *Conversations with Michael Landon.* Chicago, IL: Contemporary Books, Inc., 1992.

Landon-Wilson, Cheryl. *I Promised My Dad: An Intimate Portrait of Michael Landon By His Eldest Daughter.* Simon & Schuster, Inc., 1992.

O'Neil, Thomas. *The Emmys.* New York: Penguin Books, 1992.

ARTICLES

Bauman, Mary Ann. *Michael Landon Fan Club Newsletter* (1998-2006).

Beck, Marilyn. "Landon to Film a Bit of His Life," Associated Press, October 4, 1976.

Beck, Marilyn. "Michael Landon Feels No Guilt in Hiring Daughter," Chicago Tribune, November 28, 1982.

Buck, Jerry. "Landon Produces Family Shows," Associated Press, March 17, 1985.

Buck, Jerry. "Reunion of *Bonanza* Stars Was 'Heaven' Sent," Associated Press, November 19, 1985.

"Cancer Center Named for Michael Landon," Los Angeles Times, July 14, 1992.

Christian, Vicki. *Bonanza Gold* (2003-2007).

Darrach, Brad and Michael Landon. "I Want to See My Kids Grow Up," Saturday Evening Post, June 1991.

Davidson, Bill. "Michael Landon, General Contractor," TV Guide, December 7, 1974.

Davidson, Bill. "It Was Michael Landon Against the Director," TV Guide, March 19, 1983.

Esterly, Glenn. "What Turned This American Villain into An Angel's Assistant?" TV Guide, December 21, 1985.

Esterly, Glenn. "From Grandfather to Grandson," TV Guide, January 27, 1990.

"For Michael Landon Happiness is a Slice of Salami," TV Guide, November 29, 1969.

Freeman, Don. "How Can You Keep Him Down On the Farm?" TV Guide, May 13, 1978.

Goldberg, Lee. "NBC's Man," Crain Communications, Inc., June 10, 1986.

Goodkind, Mike. "Michael Landon Loves Both Sides of Camera," Associated Press, August 20, 1977.

Haithman, Diane. "Michael Landon's 'Highway to Heaven" Paved With Good Intentions," Los Angeles Times, January 1988.

Inman, Julia. "Landon Compassionate Man," Indianapolis Star, April 1, 1979.

Kiester, Edwin Jr. "Big Guys Don't Cry," TV Guide, November 28, 1981.

Lewis, Richard Warren. "He Plays Cowboys and Indians for $13,000 a Week," TV Guide, July 22, 1967.

Martinez, Al and Joanne Martinez. "Linwood Boomer's Luck," TV Guide, July 14, 1979.

"Michael Landon: Out of Sight But Not Out of Mind," The TV Collector, November-December, 1991.

"Michael Landon Tribute," TV Guide, September 14, 1991.

Mitchell, Lisa. "Michael Landon: Big Man in a 'Little House,'" Saturday Evening Post, September 1980.

Murphy, Mary. "First Rule of the Prairie: Michael Landon *Must* Have Control," TV Guide, January 9, 1982.

Episode Index

"A Child of God": 37, 128-129
"A Christmas They Never Forgot": 88
"A Dream to Dream": 34, 79
"A Harvest of Friends": 53
"A Match Made in Heaven": 129
"A Matter of Circumstance": 37
"A Most Precious Gift": 73
"A Poor Man's Treasure": 44
"A Promise to Keep": 89
"A Rose for Lotta": 29
"A Wiser Heart": 87
"Alias Joe Cartwright": 32
"All the Colors of the Heart": 140
"Alone": 131
"As Long as We're Together": 74
"At the End of the Rainbow": 60

"Back to School": 80
"Ballad of the Ponderosa": 32-33
"Bandits, Thieves and Kidnappers": 39
"Bank Run": 30
"Barn Burner": 78
"Barnaby": 44
"Be My Friend": 72-73
"Between Heaven and Earth": 32

"Blizzard": 68
"Blood Tie": 33
"Bullet for a Bride": 32
"Bunny": 62-63, 67, 68
"By the Bear That Bit Me": 105

"Calamity Over the Comstock": 32
"Castoffs": 69, 70
"Catch a Falling Star": 127-128
"Chicago": 87
"Come Let Us Reason Together": 85
"Crossed Connections": 82

"Dance with Me": 78
"Dark Star": 30
"Darkness is My Friend": 82
"Day of the Dragon": 30
"Day of Vengeance": 22
"Days of Sunshine, Days of Sorrow": 89
"Dead Wrong": 36, 106
"Dear Albert, I'll Miss You": 84-85
"Decision at Los Robles": 36-37
"Decision": 15
"Deputy Sheriff": 18
"Divorce, Walnut Grove Style": 84

"Don't Cry, My Son": 40, 44

"Eggs, Milk and a Dry Bed": 105
"End of a Young Gun": 21-22

"Fagin": 76-77
"Fight for the Title": 18, 21
"Fight, Team, Fight!": 84
"Five into the Wind": 32
"Five Sundowns to Sunup": 32
"For the Love of Blanche": 112
"For the Love of Larry": 133-34, 137
"Forever": 8, 41-44, 54, 55, 139
"Freedom Flight": 72
"Friends": 132-133

"Gambini the Great": 87
"Gift from a Gunman": 19
"Going Home": 61-62
"Going Home, Going Home": 23
"Gold Country": 68, 72

"He Loves Me, He Loves Me Not": 83
"He Was Only Seven": 40-41, 89
"He Was Only Twelve": 89-90
"Heaven Only Nose": 137
"Heavy Date": 136-137
"Hello and Goodbye": 112-113
"His Father's Son": 60
"Home Again": 111-112
"Hoss and the Leprechauns": 105

"I Was a Middle-Aged Werewolf": 138-139
"I'll Be Waving as You Drive Away": 73-74

"I'll Ride the Wind": 68
"Invention of a Gunfighter": 32
"It's a Lot of Bull": 33-34
"It's a Small World": 36, 44, 111

"Joe Cartwright, Detective": 33
"John Michael Murphy, R.I.P.": 106
"Johnny Risk": 20
"Journey in the Spring": 63-64, 68, 69
"Keep Smiling;": 131, 139
"Kingdom of Fear": 38

"Laura Ingalls Wilder": 83-84
"Little Girl Lost": 63
"Little Lou": 36, 111
"Living is a Lonesome Thing": 23, 114
"Love Came Laughing": 48

"Man's Best Friend": 137
"Marvin's Garden": 111
"May We Make Them Proud": 82-83
"Merry Christmas from Grandpa": 142-143
"Mr. Edwards' Homecoming": 53
"My Ellen": 70

"Night of Reckoning": 33
"No Beast So Fierce": 88

"One Fresh Batch of Lemonade": 129

"Peace Officer": 32
"Plague": 55

"Plane Death": 128
"Portrait of Love": 84
"Pride of a Man": 33

"Quarantine": 68

"Remember Me": 8, 56-60, 64, 104, 106, 139
"Ride the Wind": 24, 32
"Rose of the Rio Bravo": 21

"Sam Bass": 20
"Shadows of Belle Starr": 23
"Shotgun Messenger": 20
"Showdown at Tahoe": 34
"Silent Thunder": 30
"Six Black Horses": 33
"Someone Please Love Me": 34, 79
"Sylvia": 85-86, 87, 112

"Terror at 2:00": 37-38
"That's Our Dad": 133
"The Award": 53
"The Code": 32
"The Collection": 62, 68
"The Conquistadors": 33
"The Craftsman": 77, 123
"The Devil and Jonathan Smith": 138
"The Dream Day": 106
"The Fighter": 71-72
"The First Born": 32
"The Friendship": 30
"The Gamble": 30-31
"The Giant Killer": 44
"The Gift": 30
"The Godsister": 77
"The Gunmen": 30

"The Halloween Dream": 81
"The Heir Apparent": 106
"The Hemp Tree": 22
"The Hero": 135-136
"The High Price of Being Right": 71
"The Hunter": 45
"The Hunters": 65, 68
"The Julia Bulette Story": 29
"The Kid": 20
"The King is Dead": 82
"The Lake Kezia Monster": 78
"The Last Assignment": 132
"The Last Haircut": 32
"The Last Hunt": 30
"The Legacy": 88
"The Legend": 23-24
"The Lonely House": 30
"The Long Road Home": 60-61
"The Lord is My Shepherd": 54-55, 73, 139
"The Lost Ones": 86
"The Love Child": 37, 44, 64, 128
"The Man from Brewster": 24
"The Man Inside": 74-75
"The Martin Poster": 21
"The Mind Reader": 24
"The Mountain Girl": 30
"The Music Box": 67-68
"The Newcomers": 65
"The Odyssey": 79
"The Older Brothers": 111
"The Passing of a King": 35
"Playing for Keeps": 137
"The Pueblo Kid": 21
"The Quality of Mercy": 32
"The Quest": 32
"The Reincarnation of Nellie": 87

"The Restless Gun" (episode): 19
"The Return of Mr. Edwards": 81
"The Richest Man in Walnut Grove": 56
"The Right Thing": 129-130
"The Secret": 30
"The Silent Cry": 45, 84
"The Smile in the Third Row": 130-131
"The Sound of Sadness": 44. 84
"The Spy": 105
"The Squeaky Wheel": 142
"The Stillness Within": 38-39
"The Storm": 7, 30
"The Stranger": 73
"The Swordsman": 18
"The Third Miracle": 80-81
"The Tin Badge": 30
"The Trap": 32
"The Twenty-Sixth Grave": 44
"The Unwanted": 44
"The Wedding": 77
"The Wisdom of Solomon": 68
"The Wish": 35-36
"The Wormwood Cup": 33
"The Younger Brothers' Younger Brother": 41, 111
"There's No Place Like Home": 75-76
"Times Are Changing": 110-111
"To Die in Darkness": 34-35
"To Live with Fear": 68
"To Run and Hide": 71
"To See the Light": 85
"To See the World": 55
"To Touch the Moon": 126-127
"Top Hand": 52
"Twilight Town": 32

"Wally": 134-135
"Way of the West": 20
"We Have Forever": 139-140
"Whatever Happened to the Class of '56": 82
"Whisper Country": 72
"White Warrior": 20

GENERAL INDEX

A&E: 144
A Christmas Carol: 142
Abbott, Chris: 87, 89
ABC: 44, 68, 69, 86, 104, 112, 130, 133, 137, 141
Adams, Nick: 21
Age Old Friends: 146
Albertson, Jack: 44
Alcoa Theater: 19, 20
All in the Family: 44
Allen, Rex: 23
Anderson, Melissa (Sue): 4, 51, 67, 73, 87, 88, 146
Anderson, Susan: 22
Apple's Way: 51
Arngrim, Alison: 4, 51, 63
Asner, Ed: 132
Atterbury, Malcom: 19
Ayers, Lew: 20, 129

Baddeley, Hermione: 70, 78
Baer, Parley: 106
Ball, Lucille: 150
Balluck, Don: 71, 77, 78, 82, 84, 86, 88, 89, 112
Balson, Allison: 87
Barry, Donald "Red": 52, 78

Bartlett, Bonnie: 57, 81
Bartlett, Hall: 113
Barty, Billy: 111
Bateman, Jason: 86
Batman: 33
Bedelia, Bonnie: 42, 44, 48
Bellamy, Ralph: 111
Bethune, Ivy: 104
Bishop, Ron: 105
Bissell, Whit: 19
Blees, Robert: 33
Bleifer, John: 123, 124
Bless All the Dear Children: 116
Blocker, Dan: 7, 28, 29, 31, 39, 41-42, 44, 52, 69
Blocker, Dirk: 52
Boggs, Haskell "Buzzy": 5, 146
Bolger, Ray: 75-76, 78
Bonanza: 5, 7, 8, 9, 15, 18, 19, 20, 24, 27-45, 48, 49, 50, 51, 52, 54, 55, 61, 64, 65, 68, 73, 74, 79, 84, 89, 105, 106, 111, 124, 128, 130, 139, 151
Bonanza: The Next Generation: 131
Boomer, Linwood: 74, 88
Boone, Randy: 32
Borgnine, Ernest: 55

Born Free: 51
Branded: 49
Brenlin, George: 18, 21
Brennan, Eileen: 48
Brinegar, Paul: 65
Bronson, Charles: 20
Browne, Roscoe Lee: 40
Buchanan, Edgar: 20
Bull, Richard: 5, 52, 110
Butler, Dean: 80

Cagney, James: 18
Caldwell, Erskine: 23
Calhoun, Rory: 22
Campanella, Roy: 48
Campbell, R. Wright: 146
Canary, David: 33, 38, 42
Cannon, Katherine: 104
Capra, Frank: 123
Carey, Philip: 81
Carney, Art: 146
Carradine, John: 24, 36
Carson, Johnny: 149
Carter Country: 68, 69, 81
Cash, Johnny: 62
Cash, June Carter: 62
Casper, Robert: 112
Cavalcade of America: 18
CBS: 44, 69, 143, 147, 150
Charles in Charge: 124
Charro!: 50
Chen, Moira: 114
Cheyenne: 15, 18, 20
Chinquy, Ron: 72
Chordettes, The: 117
Clauser, Suzanne: 38
Claxton, William F.: 33, 34, 53, 55, 76, 79, 83, 84, 105, 106

Cleaver, Frank: 31
Cole, Nat King: 117
Combat!: 33
Connor, Lawrence M.: 71
Connors, Chuck: 20, 21, 22,
Conway, Pat: 21
Cooper, Paul W.: 63, 89, 142
Cosby, Bill: 8
Crawford, Johnny: 22, 65
Crawford, Oliver: 33
Cromwell, James: 84
Cronyn, Hume: 146
Crossroads: 15, 18
Crusader: 66
Culp, Robert: 21

Dallas: 86
Daniel Boone: 50
Darrach, Brad: 150
Davis, Ossie: 35
Day, Gerry: 55
De Carlo, Yvonne: 29
De Kova, Frank: 81
Debussy, Claude: 132, 139
Dexter, Joy: 33
Dexter, Maury: 106, 110
Dick Powell's Zane Grey Theater: 19, 23, 114
Doherty, Shannen: 105, 110
Dortort, David: 4, 7, 10, 28-29, 30, 31, 33, 34, 35, 39, 41, 42, 44, 130-31, 150
Doyle, Robert: 61
Dragnet: 33
Dreams: 124
Duffy, Patrick: 151
Dugan, John T.: 71, 78, 80, 82
Dunn, Michael: 36

DuPont Theater: 18
Dynasty: 133, 141

Edds, Hank: 72, 138
Edwards, James: 14
Elam, Jack: 105
Emmich, Cliff: 75
Everingham, John: 113, 114

Falcon Crest: 86
Father Murphy: 33, 86, 103-107, 111, 150
Fenady, Andy: 49
Ferrone, Dan: 44
Flippen, Lucy Lee: 80, 84, 87, 89
Flynn, Harry: 3, 4
Flynn, Pamela: 3
Forbes, Scott: 18
Ford, John: 77
Ford, Mary: 117
Four Aces, The: 117
Francis, Missy: 86
French, Ted: 50
French, Victor: 50, 52, 59, 68-69, 81, 87, 88, 89, 110, 111, 112, 122, 128, 142
Friedman, David: 110
Friendly, Ed: 49, 50
Frontier Doctor: 23

Geer, Will: 37
Gehring, Ted: 52, 56
General Electric Theater: 18
Germain, Larry: 85
Get Smart: 50
Gibbs, Timothy: 104
Gilbert, Melissa: 4, 51, 110, 112, 150

God's Little Acre: 23
Golden, Larry: 42, 61
Gordon, Leo: 82
Gorman, Robert Hy: 145
Gossett, Lou: 49, 61
Grassle, Karen: 52, 110, 115, 151
Greenbush, Billy: 52
Greenbush, Lindsay: 52, 77
Greenbush, Sidney: 52, 77
Greene, Lorne: 28, 29, 31, 37, 41-42, 44, 53, 130-131
Greer, Dabbs: 21, 52
Greer, Jane: 29
Gunn, Moses: 5, 71, 104
Gunsmoke: 7, 24, 28, 41, 50, 81, 105
Gutierrez, Vince R.: 82, 88, 89

Hackett, Buddy: 23
Hagen, Kevin: 5, 20, 52
Haggerty, Don: 18
Hanalis, Blanche: 50
Happy Days: 104, 112
Harmon, Estelle: 14
Harris, Julie: 34
Harrison, Susan: 30
Hawaii Five-O: 44
Hawkins, John: 32, 53, 60, 68, 72, 87
Hayes, Alan: 117
Hayes, Helen: 124
Hayes, Steve: 105
HBO: 146
Head of the Class: 137
Heaven Can Wait: 123, 140
Heckart, Eileen: 78
Heinemann, Arthur: 62, 73, 77, 81
Here Comes Mr. Jordan: 123

High School Confidential: 22-23
Highway to Heaven: 5, 8, 18, 19, 20, 23, 37, 121-144, 148
Hill, Arthur: 63
Hogan, Jack: 24
Home of the Brave: 14
Hope, Bob: 137
Hud: 56
Hunley, Leann: 141
Hunnicutt, Arthur: 36
Hunter, Kenneth: 80
Hutchinson, Josephine: 37

I Was a Teenage Werewolf: 19, 138
Inhat, Steve: 34
Ireland, John: 63
It's A Wonderful Life: 123
It's Good to Be Alive: 48-49
Ito, Tom: 4, 11, 105
Ivar, Stan: 110, 137
Ives, Burl: 65

Jackson, Anne: 117
Jaeckel, Richard: 61
Jenson, Roy: 42
Jericho: 114
Jerome, William: 33
Jeter, James: 52
Johnny Staccato: 23
Johnson, Rafer: 67
Johnson, Don: 131
Jones, Claude Earl: 88
Jory, Victor: 23-24

Karen, James: 115, 118
Kayden, Tony: 70
Keith, Brian: 66
Kennedy, Lindsay: 110

Kerwin, Lance: 66
Keys, William: 55
King, Larry: 143
King, Martin Luther: 36, 38
Kingston Trio, The: 24
Korn, Dennis: 3, 147
Kung Fu: 50

Laborteaux, Matthew: 64, 69, 74, 129
Laborteaux, Patrick: 69
Lamarr, Hedy: 118
Lancer: 135
Landon, Cindy: 3, 4, 5, 8, 151
Landon, Jennifer: 143, 148
Landon, Jr., Michael: 131, 150
Landon, Leslie: 55, 80, 87, 106, 110
Landon, Mark: 42, 148
Lassie: 50
Laurents, Arthur: 14
Laverne and Shirley: 104
Lawson, Carol: 37, 44
Lear, Norman: 44
Lee, Joanna: 117
Little House on the Prairie: 5, 8, 13, 20, 21, 32, 33, 34, 37, 45, 47-90, 104, 106, 110, 111, 112, 113, 122, 123, 124, 130, 139, 148, 150
Little House: A New Beginning: 20, 36, 51, 106, 109-116
Look Back to Yesterday: 114
Lord, Jack: 23
Louise, Tina: 23
Love is Forever: 113-114
Love Story: 48
Luke and the Tenderfoot: 20

General Index

Lynch, Ken: 24

MacGregor, Katherine: 52, 110
Maltin, Leonard: 67
Mann, Anthony: 23
Mannix: 50
Maracaibo: 22
Martin, Barney: 148, 150
Martin, Strother: 41
Matheson, Tim: 42
Matinee Theatre: 19
Mature, Victor: 14, 118
Maude: 44
Mazurki, Mike: 36
McCray, Kent: 33, 68-69, 85, 123, 147, 151
McCray, Susan: 3, 51, 67, 123
McGuire, Dorothy: 131-132, 139
McQueen, Steve: 21, 23
Mears, DeAnn: 66
Mellini, Scott: 104
Memories of Laughter and Love: 150
Mercer, Johnny: 117
Meredith, Burgess: 33
Meredith, Cheerio: 24
Miami Vice: 131
Michael Landon: The Father I Knew: 150
Mission: Impossible: 50
Mitchum, Jim: 61
Moody, Ralph: 24
Morrow, Jo: 24
Morrow, Vic: 23
Murcott, Joel: 53
Murphy, Brianne: 123, 129
Murphy, Timothy Patrick: 117, 119

Name That Tune: 67

NBC: 28, 29, 30, 33, 41, 44, 50, 60, 62, 64, 65, 68, 69, 74, 106, 112, 113, 117, 122, 123, 141, 146, 147, 150, 151
Neal, Patricia: 56, 57, 60
Nicholson, Jack: 19
Nimoy, Leonard: 20
Nolan, Kathy: 21

O'Connor, Donald: 137
O'Connor, John J.: 123
O'Kun, Lan: 130
O'Neill, Kathleen Peggy: 12
Old Yeller: 133
Olsen, Merlin: 5, 69, 82, 86, 104, 150
Orowitz, Eli: 12-13, 15, 29
Orowitz, Evelyn: 12, 14

Parady, Hersha: 69
Passing Parade: 15
Paul, Les: 117
Payne, John: 19, 28
Perry Mason: 30
Peterson, Casey: 148
Pevney, Joseph: 38, 106
Playhouse 90: 23
Pollack, Dee: 24
Ponderosa: 41
Post, Ted: 24
Prochnow, Jurgen: 114
Promised Land: 143
Putnam, William: 53

Quillan, Eddie: 106
Quinn, Bill: 61
Quist, Gerald: 138

Raison, Bob: 15
Raschella, Carole: 73, 76, 79, 85, 88
Raschella, Michael: 73, 76, 79, 85, 88
Rawhide: 50, 65
Ray, Aldo: 23
Rennie, Michael: 23
Rhodes, Michael: 111
Richards, Kyle: 81
Ride Lonesome: 28
Rio Lobo: 50
Roberts, Pernell: 28, 32
Robinson, Andy: 42
Rose, David: 37, 40, 43, 52, 55, 60, 65, 67, 77, 86, 89, 123, 128
Route 66: 123, 148
Roylance, Pamela: 110, 116
Russell, Bing: 36, 67
Rust, Richard: 24
Ryan, Robert: 23

Sam's Son: 13, 117-119
Samson and Delilah: 14, 118
Sandefur, B.W.: 68, 87
Schlitz Playhouse of Stars: 19, 20
Schneider, John: 150
Scott, Randolph: 28
Scovell, Jane: 4
Seinfeld: 148
Sen Yung, Victor: 32
Sharp, Alex: 151
Silliphant, Stirling: 22
Sirisomphone, Keo: 113
Skerritt, Tom: 45
Slate, Jeremy: 35
Snodgress, Carrie: 127
Snyder, Allan: 72

Sons and Daughters: 51
Sorrells, Robert: 36
Spain, Fay: 23
Spielberg, David
St. Jacques, Raymond: 71
Stacy, James: 135
Stanwyck, Barbara: 18
State Trooper: 18
Stewart, Charlotte: 52
Stir Crazy: 130
Stowe, Madeline: 84
Studio One: 20
Suspicion: 19
Swanton, Harold: 65
Swenson, Karl: 52, 76

Tales of Wells Fargo: 20
Tartikoff, Brandon: 122, 123, 147
Taylor, Dub: 84
Taylor, Jeri: 87
Tea and Sympathy: 15
Teal, Ray: 18, 20
Telephone Time: 18
That's Incredible: 86, 112
The 20th Century-Fox Hour: 18
The Adventures of Jim Bowie: 18
The Bat: 14
The Bishop's Wife: 123
The Court of Last Resort: 19
The Dakotas: 50
The Fall Guy: 124
The High Chaparral: 33
The Horn Blows at Midnight: 123
The Insiders: 130
The Jackie Robinson Story: 48
The Jeffersons: 86
The Last Farewell: 114-116, 117
The Lawrence Welk Show: 141

General Index

The Legend of Tom Dooley: 24
The Loneliest Runner: 65-67, 88, 117
The Magnificent Seven: 50
The Most Dangerous Game: 45
The Real McCoys: 21
The Rebel: 21, 49
The Restless Gun (series): 19, 28
The Rifleman: 7, 20, 21-22, 24, 65
The San Pedro Beach Bums: 69
The Texan: 20, 22
The Tonight Show: 149
The Virginian: 50
The Waltons: 50, 51, 62
The Wizard of Oz: 76
These Wilder Years: 18
Three's Company: 86
Tobin, Michele: 34
Todd, Hallie: 118
Tombstone Territory: 20, 24
Touched by an Angel: 143
Trackdown: 20, 21, 22
Tracy, Steve: 83
Troesh, James: 129
Troesh, Theresa: 129
Trusel, Lisa: 104
Tuesday Movie of the Week: 44
Two Faces West: 50
Tyner, Charles: 104, 105, 111

U.S. Marshal: 23
Us: 49, 147-149, 150

Van Cleef, Lee: 20

Van Dyke, Dick: 134
Van Fleet, Jo: 38
Viscott, David: 12
Vogel, Mitch: 40, 52, 55
Voigtlander, Ted: 5, 48, 52, 60, 72, 77, 82, 86, 89, 123, 129
Vollaerts, Rik: 32

Wagon Train: 28, 30
Walker, Clint: 20
Wallach, Eli: 117, 119
Walston, Ray: 82
Wanted Dead or Alive: 20, 21, 23-24
Welles, Orson: 1, 77
Westmore, Michael: 138
Where Pigeons Go to Die: 8, 146-147
Where There's a Will, There's an A: 13-14
Whitaker, Jonnie: 34
Whitmore, James: 34
Wilde, Cornel: 22
Wilder, Laura Ingalls: 49, 50
Williams, Guy: 19
Wilson, Cheryl Landon: 4, 48
Windom, William: 128
Winfield, Paul: 48
Wire Service: 18
Witney, William: 23, 31
Wixted, Michael-James: 37
Wolff, Paul: 77, 78

Young Dan'l Boone: 69

The Legend of Tom Dooley: 24
The Loneliest Runner: 65-67, 88, 117
The Magnificent Seven: 50
The Most Dangerous Game: 45
The Real McCoys: 21
The Rebel: 21, 49
The Restless Gun (series): 19, 28
The Rifleman: 7, 20, 21-22, 24, 65
The San Pedro Beach Bums: 69
The Texan: 20, 22
The Tonight Show: 149
The Virginian: 50
The Waltons: 50, 51, 62
The Wizard of Oz: 76
These Wilder Years: 18
Three's Company: 86
Tobin, Michele: 34
Todd, Hallie: 118
Tombstone Territory: 20, 24
Touched by an Angel: 143
Trackdown: 20, 21, 22
Tracy, Steve: 83
Troesh, James: 129
Troesh, Theresa: 129
Trusel, Lisa: 104
Tuesday Movie of the Week: 44
Two Faces West: 50
Tyner, Charles: 104, 105, 111

U.S. Marshal: 23
Us: 49, 147-149, 150

Van Cleef, Lee: 20

Van Dyke, Dick: 134
Van Fleet, Jo: 38
Viscott, David: 12
Vogel, Mitch: 40, 52, 55
Voigtlander, Ted: 5, 48, 52, 60, 72, 77, 82, 86, 89, 123, 129
Vollaerts, Rik: 32

Wagon Train: 28, 30
Walker, Clint: 20
Wallach, Eli: 117, 119
Walston, Ray: 82
Wanted Dead or Alive: 20, 21, 23-24
Welles, Orson: 1, 77
Westmore, Michael: 138
Where Pigeons Go to Die: 8, 146-147
Where There's a Will, There's an A: 13-14
Whitaker, Jonnie: 34
Whitmore, James: 34
Wilde, Cornel: 22
Wilder, Laura Ingalls: 49, 50
Williams, Guy: 19
Wilson, Cheryl Landon: 4, 48
Windom, William: 128
Winfield, Paul: 48
Wire Service: 18
Witney, William: 23, 31
Wixted, Michael-James: 37
Wolff, Paul: 77, 78

Young Dan'l Boone: 69

About the Author

David R. Greenland has been writing professionally for more than forty years. His work has appeared in numerous newspapers and magazines, including *Classic Images*, to which he contributes the monthly "What's Out There" column. He is the author of *Bonanza: A Viewer's Guide to the TV Legend*, *Rawhide: A History of Television's Longest Cattle Drive* and *Gunsmoke: A New History of Television's Greatest Western*, all published by BearManor Media. In addition, he is the ghostwriter of two books by other authors, and co-author of *Inside the Fire: My Strange Days with the Doors* by B. Douglas Cameron. David and his wife, Cleo, live in Illinois with Chloe, their sixth dog.

www.ingramcontent.com/pod-product-compliance
Lightning Source LLC
Chambersburg PA
CBHW062003180426
43198CB00036B/2171